John Tovey's

ENTERTAINING on a plate!

OTHER BOOKS BY JOHN TOVEY:
Entertaining with Tovey
Table Talk with Tovey
Food and Flowers for the Four Seasons (co-authored by Derek Bridges)
Feast of Vegetables
The Miller Howe Cookbook
Country Weekends
Wicked Puddings
Eating Out with Tovey
Radio Times Step-by-Step All-Colour Cookbook

John Tovey's
ENTERTAINING
~on a plate!

BBC BOOKS

Published by BBC Books,
a division of BBC Enterprises Limited,
Woodlands, 80 Wood Lane, London W12 0TT

First published 1991
© John Tovey 1991
ISBN 0 563 36199 9

Edited by Susan Fleming
Designed by Sara Kidd
Illustrations by Angela McAllister
Photographs by Martin Brigdale
Styling by Andrea Lambton
Home Economist Margaret Armstrong

Set in Bembo by Ace Filmsetting Ltd, Frome, Somerset
Printed and bound in Great Britain by Clays Ltd, St Ives plc
Colour separations by Technik Ltd, Berkhamstead
Jacket printed by Belmont Press Ltd, Northampton

All recipes (bar some in the Buffet section) are for six people.

CONTENTS

INTRODUCTION

This book, and the television series which it accompanies have been created to help revive the dying art of entertaining at home. How often, when you have guests coming, does your heart sink at the thought of all the work involved? I want to make that sinking feeling a thing of the past, to take away the agony, replacing it with a little ecstasy! *Any* cooking, however simple, does involve some work though, but if you plan your entertaining occasion properly, everything becomes easy. Tovey's first law of entertaining is to prepare in advance and to be organised. If you're organised, you're confident, and if you're confident, half the battle is won.

As a result, all the entertaining occasions in this book – three lunches or dinners per season, plus a vegetarian buffet and a brunch – have been designed so that a major proportion of the work involved can be done in advance. And to help you plan this, I have written countdowns for each party, detailing when things ought to be done. Party day is designated D-Day, so if D-Day is on a Wednesday, D-Day Minus Two instructions mean you start work on the Monday! I've done this so that you will be aware of what tasks can be done ahead of time, and to allow you, on D-Day itself, to spend as much time as possible with your guests, and to be relaxed, friendly and happy!

I have also written shopping lists of everything needed for that particular meal. The lists might seem a little foolish at first, because they give *exact* ingredients but they are a *guide* to what you need to have before you start.

Another area which often causes nervousness is the table setting. To avoid any last-minute panic, do this the day before if you can: lay out the cloth or place mats, arrange the cutlery, and put the glasses in place, but upside down. *Vary* the look of your table as much as you like – with differing colours of inexpensive cloths and accessories, flowers, containers, and diverse decorations – I use cherubs, semi-precious stones, anything that takes my fancy!

For cloths, I buy seconds or end of rolls of fabric from the market, and hem them to fit the table. The china needn't be the finest Wedgwood either; I buy bits and pieces whenever I see anything that catches my eye, and if there's one plate short or chipped, I don't let that worry me. The flower container could be anything from a cracked china soup tureen, to a set of cake stands. One hint about flowers: don't use any that are *too* heavily scented on the table. And if you use candles, they must always be lit!

Cooking is a form of loving, and with this book by your side, I hope that you will learn how to make impressive, delicious and, above all, easy meals, and that entertaining will become as much fun for you as for your guests.

SPRING

I love spring. As the days start to grow longer and the temperature rises, I take to the fells or moors to walk my dog Ozzie with renewed vigour. And it's there that I encounter the sheep that form the main meat theme of my three spring parties. However, always buy lamb that is a year old – born last spring – which is far tastier and much better value. I like Lakeland Herdwick or Welsh lamb, and it should have been hung for at least three weeks to allow the flavours and texture to develop.

As for the table settings, green is the colour of spring for me. I like to mix and match my green in the plates and flower arrangement with creamy-white cloths and napkins. There's no shortage of seasonal flowers now, and I use a scattering of semi-precious stones as an original talking point! I am not averse to sprinkling freshly picked wild daffodils all over the table.

WINES FOR SPRING PARTIES

A Chardonnay to go with each of the starters, a good New World Cabernet Sauvignon with all the lamb dishes, and a glass of chilled Frangelico and crushed ice with each of the puds!

Seek out a good-coloured, buttery Chardonnay, and my personal favourite, although at the top end of the price range, is the Orlando St Hilary from Australia. They have good wines in a lower price range too, and you will not be disappointed by the younger straight Orlando or a Stoneleigh Marlborough Chardonnay from New Zealand. If you prefer your Chardonnays slightly drier, seek one blended with the Sémillon grape.

You will be spoilt for choice by the Cabernet Sauvignons proudly produced down under. New Zealand has its Matua and Nobilo wines, and Australia its Hill-Smith, the Orlando again, as well as Peterson which comes high up on my list.

Frangelico is a tantalising liqueur made in Italy from hazelnuts and wild herbs. Seek the monk-shaped bottle out, and I am sure it will become a firm favourite in your drinks cupboard. It's particularly good served with the farmhouse pie, and magnificent with summer fruits as well!

Spring Menu One

Spinach Croûton Nest with Baby Potatoes,
Bacon and Hot Walnut Orange Dressing

•

Roast Leg of Lamb with Coriander,
Garlic and Rosemary
accompanied by
Tomato Provençale (see p. 251)
Aubergine Pepper Custard
Rösti Potatoes
Gravy (see p. 249)

•

Pear, Macadamia and Ginger Farmhouse Pie

---

*A*lthough this looks like a fairly labour-intensive menu, you will have started your preparation at least 2 days before and on the day itself you will have plenty of time to make everything look good. Very little is left until the last minute, so you will be able to enjoy your guests' company and share with them the wine you will be opening. I think the menu will have your guests – and you – singing like the birds that return in spring!

The major 'lesson' of my spring entertaining occasions is that of making Farmhouse pastry; you'll find the recipe for this on p. 244. It is a rich and satisfying pastry which I know, once you've mastered it, you'll be able to use for many different pies. At the hotel and at the farm I've used tinned black cherries with rum; banana, walnut and dates; pears with Stilton cheese; and blackberries and apples in the autumn – the variations are virtually endless. Never make this pastry – or indeed any of the others – when you're having a nark; you must be relaxed and happy, so do it while listening to your favourite cassette or radio programme.

Many people are reluctant to serve a roast at a dinner party, thinking it will take time to carve (or lacking confidence in their carving ability) – and then there's the gravy, vegetables, etc. However, by making the gravy ahead of time you'll get that out of the way, and if you follow my instructions about the lamb, the whole thing will be very simple indeed. You can carve it in the privacy of the kitchen, out of sight of all your guests, and then serve it up later with consummate ease!

Spinach croûton nest with baby potatoes, bacon and hot walnut orange dressing

I like to have an element of surprise/shock/sensation when entertaining, as that is what good theatre is all about. Whenever I serve this dish my guests' faces break into such lovely smiles as they see what I am trying to get at – a bird's nest with new-laid eggs! Aah, you might say – but it does work, and it breaks any ice there might be at the beginning of a party.

36 large spinach leaves, well washed and tough stalks removed
freshly grated nutmeg
a little sea salt and freshly ground black pepper
18–24 unpeeled mini new potatoes or about 1 ¾ lb (800 g) old potatoes, peeled and turned with a Parisian scoop

a little freshly squeezed lemon juice
6 Large-base croûtons (see p. 248)
4 oz (100 g) smoked bacon, rinded and finely diced
2 tablespoons walnut oil
finely grated rind and juice of 1 orange
5 fl oz (150 ml) olive oil
1 teaspoon white wine vinegar

Steam the spinach leaves in your steamer (or a colander over boiling salted water) for 2–3 minutes. Remove and pat dry on kitchen paper, spread out flat on a plastic or baking tray and season with the nutmeg, salt and pepper. When cold, cover with cling film and put in the fridge. This can be done in the morning.

If you are fortunate enough to obtain the first of the season's new potatoes, just wash them (never peel as most of the flavour is in the skin) and cook in simmering salted water until *just* tender. If you can't get these, use

Previous page: Cool blue-grey and a touch of red for a spring lunch or dinner party. The starter is a Spinach croûton nest with baby potatoes, bacon and hot walnut orange dressing.

old peeled potatoes, make balls with your Parisian scoop and cook in the same fashion. Strain and then put in a basin and cover with cold water and a little fresh lemon juice. This too can be done in the morning.

Bring out your baked croûtons and arrange them on a baking tray. Arrange 6 leaves of cooked spinach in a circle around the edge of each and place 3 to 4 cooked potatoes in the middle of each.

In a small frying-pan cook the diced bacon in the walnut oil until nice and crisp. Remove the bacon from the pan with a slotted spoon and put aside until cool. Scatter the bacon over the potatoes in the nests, then cover with cling film and store in the fridge. Keep the pan with the oil and bacon fat.

When you wish to serve, simply warm the prepared croûtons through in the reduced-temperature oven after the lamb has been removed to rest. Leave for 5 or so minutes. Meanwhile, add the orange rind and juice, olive oil and vinegar to the small pan in which the bacon was previously cooked and bring quickly to the boil.

Put the croûton nests on hot plates, divide the hot dressing between them and serve immediately.

Roast leg of lamb with coriander, garlic and rosemary

—————————————————•—————————————————

If you are a lamb lover, your thoughts will probably turn immediately to *spring* lamb (seeing as this is a dinner for a spring evening), but if you buy *last year's* lamb you will be very agreeably surprised at the taste and texture of this 'muttony' dish.

1 leg of Lakeland or Welsh lamb, weighing at least 6 lb (2.75 kg) on the bone
6 fresh garlic cloves, peeled (garlic fans may go up to 12!)
12 small woody sprigs of rosemary

2 tablespoons ground coriander (preferably ground on the day)
salt and freshly ground black pepper
6 oz (175 g) soft butter

On the morning of your party take the leg of lamb out of the fridge and wipe with a clean dry cloth. Put it in a roasting tray. Make 12 deep incisions evenly over the meat, and into each put either a half or whole garlic clove (remove any green centre) and then a sprig of rosemary. The end result looks rather like a balding hedgehog! Sprinkle with the freshly ground coriander and a generous amount of salt and pepper, then spread with the soft butter. Cover with aluminium foil and put in the fridge.

When you are ready to roast the lamb, pre-heat the oven to gas mark 6, 400°F (200°C). Cook for 1½ hours in the pre-heated oven, basting from time to time. Old well-hung lamb needs this length of time as I don't personally like it bloody in the middle.

Remove from the oven, wrap in aluminium foil and leave to rest for 20 minutes or so. It won't lose its heat, and it will carve better. Carve the joint in the kitchen, slicing carefully, then reassemble the slices, cover the

Roast leg of lamb served with a wedge of Rösti potatoes, an Aubergine pepper custard, and some Tomato Provençale.

lamb again, and rest in the oven for another 20–30 minutes.

Serve the lamb slices on individual hot plates, with a dollop of Tomato provençale (see p. 251), a wedge of Rösti and the turned-out Aubergine pepper custards. Serve the Gravy (see p. 249) separately.

Aubergine pepper custard

You need six 3-in (7.5-cm) ramekins for baking these, so when you go out to buy the aubergine, remember it has to be cut in circles that will fit these dishes comfortably.

a little butter for greasing
18 × ¼-in (5-mm)-thick circles of peeled aubergine, about 3 in (7.5 cm) in diameter
5 tablespoons walnut oil

6 level tablespoons Red pepper marmalade (see p. 251)
10 fl oz (300 ml) double cream
2 free-range eggs plus 1 egg yolk
salt and freshly ground black pepper

Pre-heat the oven to gas mark 4, 350°F (180°C), and butter the 6 ramekins lightly.

Fry the aubergine circles in the heated walnut oil and leave to drain. Lay one round of aubergine on the base of each ramekin and on top of this put ½ tablespoon of the pepper marmalade. Repeat, and then top each with another aubergine round, so using a total of 3 rounds per ramekin.

Beat the cream with the eggs and extra yolk, and season with salt and pepper. Put the 6 ramekins into a small roasting tray and divide the prepared custard between them. Fill the tray with enough boiling water to come half-way up the sides of the ramekins. Cook in the pre-heated oven for 40–45 minutes. Remove from the tray and leave to settle for about 10 minutes. Run a knife around the sides to remove the custards neatly. Serve them immediately.

Rösti potatoes

Recently, when I lost 2 stone on my BBC Barry Lynch diet, I was so pleased with myself that I cooked a whole free-range chicken stuffed with Cheese and herb pâté, spread generously with butter, and ate *half* of it with 8 oz each of broad beans and garden peas from my neighbours' smallholding along with *10 oz* of these devilishly wicked spuds! I enjoyed every single mouthful and moment, but went back on the diet the next day without venturing on to the scales . . .

There are two snags with rösti: the potatoes *have* to be King Edwards, and they also have to be peeled, prepared and cooked as near to the time of serving as possible. They are well worth the effort!

> *1 lb (450 g) King Edward*
>   *potatoes*
> *3 oz (75 g) soft butter*
>
> *salt and freshly ground black*
>   *pepper*

Peel the potatoes, coarsely grate into a clean tea towel, and then wring out all the milky, starchy juices. Have half the butter at the sizzling stage in a 9-in (23-cm) frying-pan and throw in the grated potatoes. Season well and keep pressing them down very very firmly to get the criss-cross potato shreds to stick together, forming an intricate spider's web, and to brown well. At the same time keep drawing in from the outside so that you make what looks like a pancake. After 3 minutes' cooking, put the remaining butter on the top of the uncooked potatoes and, with a spatula or palette knife, flip the pancake over and repeat the process until the rösti is brown, firm and crisp.

The dish will come to no harm if left on the hob over a very low light for 20 minutes. Cut in wedges to serve.

Pear, macadamia and ginger farmhouse pie

———————————•———————————

You need to have an 8- or 10-in (20–25-cm), loose-bottomed, fluted, metal flan tin for making quiches, tarts or pies. If friends have given you a pretty porcelain one, they are no friends, as you will always get pies with a soggy bottom, and never ever remove the first portion with ease. You will get 8-12 portions from this pie!

2 lb (900 g) prepared
  Farmhouse pastry (see p. 244)
plain flour for dusting
Filling
2 heaped tablespoons semolina
6 fresh ripe pears
juice of 2 lemons
4–6 oz (100–175 g)
  macadamia nuts, toasted and
  coarsely chopped

4 kernels preserved ginger,
  finely chopped
1 tablespoon syrup from the
  preserved ginger
2 tablespoons demerara sugar
2 tablespoons Crabbie's green
  ginger wine

Make sure the pastry ball for the base is of the right texture before you roll it out. Put the circular base of the flan tin on your work surface and be generous with flour, not on the base itself but all round it. Place the pastry ball on the base, push down with your hands and gently roll it out from the middle to form a circle that will go over the edge of the base and on to the flour. Do not use pressure. Make sure the pastry overlapping the edge of the base is wide enough to go up the sides of the flan tin.

    With a palette knife, flick the outside pastry over on to that on the base. Slide the knife underneath the tin base and plonk it and the pastry into the fluted part of the tin. It is a relatively simple task then, using two thumbs, to take the overlapping pastry up the sides. As it is nice and soft, if there is the odd patch on the sides that is not covered, you can use some of the pastry left from when you flatten round the top edge to fill any gaps. As a pie,

A generous slice of Pear, macadamia and ginger farmhouse pie, served with cream.

tart or quiche can leak if the base rim is not strengthened, what I do is take any pastry dough left over, roll it into long sausages and press these all the way round the base rim. Press a large sheet of aluminium foil into the tin, taking it up the sides and over the edges. Line with ceramic baking beans and put in the fridge overnight to rest.

The next day, pre-heat the oven to gas mark 3, 325°F (160°C). Bake the pie base blind for at least 40 minutes. Take out of the oven and remove the beans and foil. If you see any signs at all of butter, put the pie base back in the oven for a few more minutes. A well-pre-baked base will never go soggy once it's baked with its filling! Leave to cool. Make sure that you have the *second* ball of pastry out of the fridge and coming round to room temperature and its correct texture.

When the base is cool, sprinkle half the semolina over it. Peel, core, quarter the pears and sprinkle with the lemon juice to stop them discolouring. Arrange them, spread out, in the pastry case. Add the toasted nuts (walnuts or Brazils make good substitutes), preserved ginger, ginger syrup, sugar and the ginger wine. Sprinkle on the remaining semolina.

The other ball of pastry should now be at room temperature. Generously spread your work surface with flour and roll the pastry *gently* into a large circle. Make sure it is large enough to cover your pie and then carefully slide a palette knife underneath the rolled pastry from both ends to make sure none of the butter has stuck to the work surface. Place your rolling pin at the top edge away from you and lift this top edge up on to the rolling pin. Quickly bring the pastry towards you over the rolling pin. Lift up, put the side nearest you on the edge of the filled pie in front of you and unroll to cover the ingredients. Use the palm of your hand to trim the edges and press with your thumb to seal lid and base together. Pop back into the fridge once more to rest and chill for at least 30 minutes.

Pre-heat the oven to gas mark 4, 350°F (180°C). Cook the pie for at least 1 hour. Leave to cool a little before turning out and portioning. To turn out, have ready a large tin or upturned basin smaller than the diameter of the flan tin. Place the base on this, knock the sides gently, and the fluted side of the tin will slip off, leaving a wondrous pie to display and serve with ease. You could accompany with some whipped double cream if you like.

SHOPPING LIST

Butcher
1 leg of lamb, at least 6 lb (2.75 kg)
  on the bone
4 oz (100 g) smoked bacon

Baker
bread for croûtons

Grocer
4 fl oz (120 ml) walnut oil
7–10 fl oz (200–300 ml) olive oil
1 teaspoon white wine vinegar
6 tablespoons sherry vinegar
1¾–2 lb (800–900 g) unsalted
  butter
5 eggs
10 fl oz (300 ml) double cream
12 oz (350 g) self-raising flour
4 oz (100 g) plain flour
4 oz (100 g) cornflour
2 tablespoons semolina
9 oz (250 g) demerara sugar
4 oz (100 g) soft brown sugar
4 oz (100 g) macadamia nuts
4 kernels preserved ginger

Greengrocer
1 lb (450 g) King Edward potatoes
18–24 tiny new potatoes or about
  1¾ lb (800 g) old potatoes
2 lb 6 oz (a good 1 kg) onions
36 large spinach leaves
14–20 garlic cloves
18 tomatoes
1–2 aubergines
3 red peppers
1 lb (450 g) mixed root vegetables
12 woody sprigs of rosemary
3 lemons
3 oranges
6 ripe pears

Off-licence
2 tablespoons Crabbie's green
  ginger wine

Store-cupboard
salt and freshly ground black
  pepper
freshly grated nutmeg
2 tablespoons freshly ground
  coriander
2 pints (1.2 litres) Home-made
  stock (see p. 249)

COUNTDOWN

D-DAY MINUS TWO
Make the Red pepper marmalade (see p. 251).
Make the Farmhouse pastry (see p. 244), wrap and chill in the fridge.

D-DAY MINUS ONE
Bake the croûtons (see p. 248), cool and store.
Make the Tomato provençale (see p. 251) and the Gravy (see p. 249).
Cool, cover and store in the fridge.
Roll the pie-base pastry out, line the tin, cover with foil and baking beans
and store in the fridge.

D-DAY
AM
Blanch the spinach leaves, cook the potatoes and fry the bacon for the
starter. Cool, then arrange on the croûtons on a baking tray. Cover with
cling film and store in the fridge.
Prepare the lamb, cover with foil and store in the fridge.
Prepare the aubergine, put in ramekins and top with the Red pepper
marmalade. Cover and store in the fridge.
Blind-bake the pie base and leave to cool. Remove the pie-top pastry from
the fridge.
PM
Prepare the pears for the pie (acidulate with lemon juice), and toast the
macadamia nuts. Roll out the pastry for the top of the pie, fill the pie and
place the top pastry on. Replace the pie in the fridge.
2½ hours before you sit down
Pre-heat the oven to gas mark 6, 400°F (200°C).
2¼ hours before you sit down
Put the lamb in to cook.
45 minutes before you sit down
Take the lamb out of the oven, cover with foil and rest for 20 minutes.
Reduce the oven temperature to gas mark 4, 350°F (180°C).

30 minutes before you sit down

Prepare the custard for the aubergines, pour into the ramekins and start cooking in the oven.

Put the farmhouse pie into the oven as well.

20 minutes before you sit down

Start heating through the Tomato provençale and the Gravy on top of the stove.

15 minutes before you sit down

Prepare the potatoes, and start cooking the Rösti. Leave in the pan over a low heat while you eat the starter.

Carve the lamb, re-assemble, re-cover with foil and put back in the oven until ready to serve.

Put plates for the starter into the oven to warm.

Pop the croûton nests into the oven for a few minutes.

Heat the dressing for the croûton nests.

Serving the starter

Put plates for the main course into the oven to warm.

Remove the aubergine custards from the oven and from the bain-marie.

Divide the nests for the starter between the individual warm plates and pour over the dressing. Eat immediately.

Serving the main course

Portion the pre-carved lamb on to the warm plates, with a wedge of Rösti, the turned-out Aubergine pepper custards and a blob of Tomato provençale. Serve the Gravy separately.

Serving the dessert

Remove the farmhouse pie from the oven and leave to rest for a few minutes before taking the flan ring off. Serve.

Spring Menu Two

Wild Mushrooms on Garlic Croûton with
Emmenthal and Herbs

•

Marinated Shoulder of Lamb with Red Wine,
Orange and Herbs
accompanied by
Spinach with Orange and Nutmeg
Purée of Carrot with Ginger
Oat Potato Croquettes

•

Rum Banana Brown Bread Cream Ice in Tulip
Cases (see p. 220)

———•———

Shoulder of lamb is un-fashionable because most people think it is a cheap cut. This is why I tend not to serve it at Miller Howe, but at home at the farm I would choose it in preference to leg any day. If it's from a year-old lamb it is succulent, sweet and so full of flavour. Your butcher should be willing to take it off the bone for you. (Always keep meat bones and use them to make rich gravies: see p. 249).

I've repeated not only the lamb theme in this party, but also the croûton theme. For so little outlay of time and money, a croûton base lends a certain sophistication to a simple starter, here marinated mushrooms. You could also top croûtons with Mushroom pâté, piped Cheese and herb pâté (see pp. 204 and 209), or, in the summer, some ratatouille. The permutations are endless, as are the shapes and cooking media of the croûtons themselves (garlic oil here, butter in the first menu). Obviously the puff pastry bases on pp. 173 and 188 could also be used in much the same way.

You can ring the changes in the vegetables too if you want. The spinach can be 'marinated' with lemon juice and rind, and the carrots can be puréed with butter and cream or, for a different flavour, a tablespoon of ground coriander seeds. The potato croquettes can, of course, be rolled in a different medium – coarse oatmeal or rolled oats, crushed cornflakes, toasted nibbed almonds or simply fresh brown or white breadcrumbs.

The cream ice is slightly rich, but so delicious. Do remember to bring it out of the freezer in good time so that it can soften a little before you serve it. And don't put it in the tulip cases too soon or they will go soggy.

Wild mushrooms on garlic croûton with Emmenthal and herbs

This dish is nicest with wild mushrooms, but could of course be made with oyster mushrooms or some of the other interesting varieties now appearing in good supermarkets throughout the year. If you cannot obtain any of these, you could substitute ordinary cultivated mushrooms but they are not quite the same.

The dish can be started the day before, then brought together on the morning of your dinner party. It then takes literally 3–4 minutes to re-heat under a hot grill.

6 slices of bread
Garlic oil (see p. 250)
10 fl oz (300 ml) dry white
  wine
4 black peppercorns
1 lb (450 g) assorted wild
  mushrooms, cleaned and
  coarsely chopped

salt and freshly ground black
  pepper
3 level tablespoons chopped
  fresh garden herbs of your
  choice
4 oz (100 g) Emmenthal
  cheese, finely grated

Pre-heat the oven to gas mark 4, 350°F (180°C).

Remove and discard the crusts from the slices of bread and make the slices into 4-in (10-cm) squares. Paint these squares with Garlic oil on both sides and put on a baking tray. Bake in the pre-heated oven for 10 minutes on each side. Leave to go cold.

Meanwhile, in a small saucepan, boil the dry white wine with the black peppercorns until reduced to half the original volume. Strain off the peppercorns, and pour the reduced wine over the chopped mushrooms in a bowl. Cover when cold and leave overnight to marinate.

Previous page: Crisp white linen for a spring dinner party. The starter is Wild mushrooms on garlic croûton with Emmenthal and herbs.

On the morning of the party, divide the drained marinated mushrooms between the cooked croûtons, season, then sprinkle with the herbs and grated cheese. Cover with cling film.

To serve, remove the cling film, then simply heat through under a very hot grill. (This dish is even better if a tablespoon of Tomato provençale – see p. 251 – is put alongside each serving.)

Marinated shoulder of lamb with red wine, orange and herbs

There is a lot of snobbishness when it comes to food and even I, at the price I charge for a set dinner at Miller Howe, feel I cannot serve this dish there. But, believe you me, I cook and serve it often when entertaining at the farm. Yes, it does tend to be fattier than other lamb joints, but it's so succulent, sweet and juicy.

1 shoulder of lamb, weighing
  3–4 lb (1.3–1.75 kg) after
  boning
salt and freshly ground black
  pepper
2 tablespoons olive oil
4 oz (100 g) butter
4 tablespoons plain flour, sifted
3 tablespoons redcurrant jelly
  (optional)
1 level dessertspoon dry English
  mustard powder (optional)
Marinade
1 bottle (1¼ pints/750 ml)
  good red wine

juice and finely grated rind of 2
  large oranges
Stuffing
3 garlic cloves, crushed with 1
  teaspoon runny salt
1 teaspoon fresh thyme leaves
1 level dessertspoon fresh
  rosemary leaves
4 oz (100 g) smoked bacon,
  finely chopped
6 oz (175 g) onions, peeled and
  finely chopped

Place the boned shoulder flat in a dish and pour the marinade ingredients over it. Cover and leave to marinate in the fridge for at least 48 hours, turning it morning and evening.

Pre-heat the oven to gas mark 5, 375°F (190°C), and prepare the stuffing by mixing the ingredients well together. Take the meat out of the marinade, retaining the latter. Dry the lamb on kitchen paper, then lay flat, the inside of the shoulder up, on your work surface. Spread the stuffing over, season liberally, then roll and tie up with string. On top of the stove heat the oil and butter together in a roasting tray that will just hold your prepared shoulder snugly. When they start to 'sing', seal the shoulder all over, getting it quite brown. Remove the meat to one side, and add the marinade to the tray, followed by the flour. Stir to amalgamate, then cook, stirring, until it thickens a little and becomes a smooth sauce.

Place the shoulder back in the tray and cover the whole tray tightly with foil. Cook in the pre-heated oven for 2 hours.

There is no need to make a gravy as the reduced, thickened wine will suffice. But I would suggest, once the shoulder is cooked and is resting, still wrapped in foil, for 15 minutes, that you beat the optional ingredients into the sauce. These add enormous flavour.

Spinach with orange and nutmeg

As soon as Mrs Wild of Winster telephones each year to say her spinach is ready in her allotment, I know spring has arrived. Many folk make faces at the very mention of the word spinach, as it conjures up all sorts of horrid, limp, soggy, slimy and tasteless memories for them. But, provided you painstakingly remove the thick, tough, middle stalks, wash the leaves thoroughly, pat dry and then follow this recipe, all these horrible thoughts will vanish from your mind.

Marinated shoulder of lamb garnished with orange segments and rosemary, served with Oat potato croquettes, Spinach with orange and nutmeg, Purée of carrot with ginger, and Gravy.

> 48 fresh spinach leaves, well
>   washed, and stalk and main
>   vein removed
> juice and finely grated rind of 1
>   orange
>
> freshly grated nutmeg to taste
> salt and freshly ground black
>   pepper

A steamer is a *must*. If you haven't got a proper stainless-steel one – a perforated container with a lid which sits in a pan – improvise with a metal colander over a pan.

With your hands mix the spinach leaves with the orange juice and rind; leave as long as possible to marinate. This is best done in a big plastic bowl. Thereafter be fairly generous with the nutmeg and seasoning.

When ready to cook, heat water until boiling in the base of the steamer (or pan). Put the drained spinach into the perforated bit, cover and steam over the boiling water for 8–10 minutes.

In a small saucepan reduce the orange juice to a thick, tacky texture and spoon over the spinach.

Purée of carrot with ginger

Carrots are often considered boring, but I always enjoy them. Cooked this way, combined with the succulent, slightly rich preserved ginger, they will make your tastebuds 'sore' but also, at the same time, warm the cockles of your heart!

> 1 lb (450 g) carrots, peeled and
>   cut into even pieces
> salt and freshly ground black
>   pepper
>
> 5 fl oz (150 ml) double cream
> 1 kernel preserved ginger,
>   chopped

Rum banana brown bread cream ice in tulip cases

In my early days at Miller Howe I could not afford the luxury of a commercial ice-cream machine, so often used to make a 'cowboy' brown bread cream ice which was simply put into the freezer in individual ramekins. Now we sport the finest Italian ice-cream maker, but at the farm I make and serve this 'updated' cream ice in Tulip cases which are well worth the effort to make (see p. 220).

If you haven't got a professional scoop, the task is made easier when using a spoon if it's first dipped each time into a basin of boiling water.

*2 medium slices of wholemeal
  bread, weighing about 4 oz
  (100 g)
2 oz (50 g) demerara sugar
4 free-range egg yolks
2 oz (50 g) soft brown sugar*

*10 fl oz (300 ml) double cream
2 large soft bananas, peeled and
  roughly chopped
4 tablespoons dark rum
6 Tulip cases (see p. 220)*

Pre-heat the oven to gas mark 3, 325°F (160°C).

Break the slices of wholemeal bread into nut-sized portions and spread over a baking tray. Mix with the demerara sugar, then bake in the pre-heated oven for 1 hour. Remove from the oven and leave to cool. Bash the caramelised bread with a rolling pin so that it is in rough pieces about the side of your little fingernail. Put to one side.

In a warmed mixing bowl, beat the egg yolks vigorously until they become pale and then, little by little, slowly add the soft brown sugar. Bring the cream to the boil (do watch it carefully as it will suddenly erupt like a volcano!) and slowly dribble it on to your egg and sugar mix, beating all the time.

Rum banana brown bread cream ice in Tulip cases.

Return to the saucepan and cook the mixture over a low heat, stirring continuously with a wooden spoon, until it starts to thicken. You are basically making a custard, so if you heat it too quickly at this stage, it will split. When thick, remove from the heat and leave to cool.

Put the cold custard into your liquidiser or food processor with the roughly chopped bananas and rum. Blend until smooth. Put the bowl and its contents into the freezer for 3 hours.

Stir the ice cream, then fold in the caramelised wholemeal bread. Put back in the freezer.

Bring the ice cream out of the freezer and store in the fridge for 30 minutes before serving in scoops in the Tulip cases.

SHOPPING LIST

Butcher
1 shoulder of lamb, 3–4 lb
  (1.3–1.75 kg) after boning
4 oz (100 g) smoked bacon

Baker
bread for croûtons
2 slices wholemeal bread

Grocer
about 10 fl oz (300 ml) olive oil
at least 8 oz (225 g) butter
5 eggs
15 fl oz (450 ml) double cream
4 oz (100 g) Emmenthal cheese
6 oz (175 g) plain flour
2 oz (50 g) demerara sugar
2 oz (50 g) soft brown sugar
4 oz (100 g) caster sugar
6 oz (175 g) Jordan's crunchy oats
1 kernel preserved ginger
3 tablespoons redcurrant jelly
  (optional)
1 level dessertspoon dry English
  mustard powder (optional)

Greengrocer
1 lb (450 g) wild mushrooms
1 lb (450 g) carrots
1½ lb (700 g) potatoes
48 fresh spinach leaves
6 oz (175 g) onions
at least 1 garlic bulb
3 tablespoons fresh garden herbs
1 teaspoon fresh thyme leaves
1 dessertspoon fresh rosemary
  leaves
3 oranges
2 large bananas

Off-licence
10 fl oz (300 ml) dry white wine
1 bottle good red wine
4 tablespoons dark rum

Store-cupboard
salt and freshly ground black
  pepper
black peppercorns
freshly grated nutmeg

COUNTDOWN

D-DAY MINUS TWO

Marinate the lamb (for at least 48 hours), covered, in the fridge, turning the meat morning and evening.

Make the cream ice.

Make the Tulip cases (see p. 220) for the cream ice and store very carefully.

D-DAY MINUS ONE

Make the croûtons, cool and store.

In the evening marinate the mushrooms for the starter.

D-DAY

AM

Marinate the spinach leaves.

Make the carrot purée, cover and store in the fridge.

Make the croquettes and store in the fridge.

Prepare the starter, cover with cling film and store in the fridge.

PM

Make the stuffing, then stuff into the lamb and store in the fridge.

2¼ hours before you sit down

Pre-heat the oven to gas mark 5, 375°F (190°C).

Seal the lamb until brown, prepare the sauce, then cover tightly with foil. Place in the oven to cook.

15 minutes before you sit down

Pre-heat the grill to very hot.

5 minutes before you sit down

Take the starter out of the fridge and place under the pre-heated grill until heated through. Put plates in the oven to heat.

Serving the starter

Remove the lamb from the oven and leave to rest still covered with the foil. Add the optional ingredients to the sauce if desired.

Put plates for the main course into the oven to heat.

Start steaming the spinach and re-heating the carrot purée.

Remove the cream ice from the freezer and put in the fridge.

Place the starters on individual plates and serve.

Serving the main course

Fry and heat the croquettes through while carving the lamb.

Re-heat the sauce.

Portion the meat, vegetables and sauce on to the warm plates.

Serving the dessert

Portion the cream ice using an ice-cream scoop or warmed spoon, and place in the Tulip cases. Serve.

Spring Menu Three

Stuffed Courgettes

•

Lamb Fillet with Water Chestnuts,
Orange Segments and Watercress
accompanied by
Cauliflower with Cheese Fondue Sauce
Baked Potato Circles

•

Simple Egg Custards with Sugared Bread
Triangles

---

*T*he countdown for this
menu has been prepared as for a lunch; if you want to serve
it as a dinner, simply transfer the timing of the things listed
to be done on the evening before to the morning of D-Day
itself. Although a few things are last-minute, the whole
party should still be trouble-free as the basics – the preparation of the meat, the pudding and garnish, and the fiddly
potato circles – will have been done well in advance. As
your guests are sitting back and exchanging remarks on how
delicious the starter was, you can be at full speed in the

kitchen bringing the main course together. Thereafter, of course, all you have to do is relax.

There are a few things which can ring the changes on the basics here. Instead of the courgettes, you could of course experiment with other vegetables capable of holding a filling – red pepper halves, hollowed-out onions or beef tomatoes, etc. And the filling could change too – try the wild mushroom mix or Mushroom pâté (see pp. 32 and 204), a ratatouille or a simple minced meat sauce.

The lamb fillet could be even more substantial if you served it on a cooked 3-in (7.5-cm) croûton (see p. 248), and you could also scatter over the dish 3 tablespoons of toasted sesame seeds (see p. 122) just as you were taking them to the table. The butter for the baked potato circles could have been infused with garlic before brushing on the slices.

The pud too could be uplifted by simply putting a table-spoon of liqueur or brandy in the base of the ramekins before filling!

Stuffed courgettes

———————•———————

These can be served hot or warm, two per person as a starter – or more per person would make a good, perhaps vegetarian, lunch. Use the remaining scooped-out flesh in a vegetable soup (see p. 120).

12 courgettes, weighing about 4 oz (100 g) each
about 8 oz (225 g) onions, peeled and finely diced
2 red peppers, seeded and finely diced
2 garlic cloves, peeled and crushed

2 oz (50 g) butter
salt and freshly ground black pepper
3 tablespoons freshly grated Parmesan cheese
2 oz (50 g) fresh breadcrumbs

Top, tail and wipe the courgettes. Score along their length with a scorer. Cut a thin slice along the length of one side of each courgette to make a firm flat base. Carefully scoop out the centres of the courgettes to make boat-like shells (use a teaspoon or a small Parisian scoop). Chop one quarter of the scooped-out flesh.

Gently fry the onions, red peppers, the chopped courgette flesh and garlic in the butter. Cook for only 4–5 minutes, stirring regularly. Season with salt and pepper.

Using a teaspoon, fill the courgette boats with the stuffing. Mix together the Parmesan and breadcrumbs before spooning generously on top of each courgette. This can be done in the morning: arrange on a greased baking tray, cool and cover with cling film and leave in the fridge.

When you wish to cook, pre-heat the oven to gas mark 4, 350°F (180°C). Bake the courgettes for 45 minutes.

Previous page: A relaxed lunch party table overlooking a sunny Windermere. The starter is Stuffed courgettes.

Lamb fillet with water chestnuts, orange segments and watercress

Whilst the lamb fillet, water chestnuts, oranges and watercress may be prepared the evening before a lunch (or the morning before a dinner), this is a last-moment stir-fry recipe which may seem labour-intensive but which in fact is done very quickly indeed.

2 tablespoons olive oil
2 oz (50 g) soft butter
2 oz (50 g) onions, peeled and
  finely chopped
1 lb 2 oz (500 g) lamb fillet,
  trimmed and cut into ½-in
  (1-cm) cubes
salt and freshly ground black
  pepper

12 canned water chestnuts,
  drained and coarsely chopped
3 oranges, peeled and segmented
  (see below)
the leaves of 1 bunch of
  watercress, washed and dried

Heat the oil and butter in a frying-pan and fry the onions until golden, about 10 minutes. Turn up the heat and put in the lamb fillet whilst the heat is very high. Stir and seal, and stir-fry for 4 minutes. Season lightly.

Add the water chestnuts and stir to warm them through and lightly brown. Fold in the orange segments, cook until just warm, then turn the whole thing out on to warmed individual serving plates. Garnish with the washed and dried watercress.

Segmenting Oranges
Top and tail the fruit with a sharp knife. Cut down on a board to remove skin and pith completely. (Remember to squeeze the juice from the fleshy bits of peel.) Over a sieve over a bowl, cut down into the orange towards the centre, between flesh and membrane – *along* one side of the white line marking the segment divisions. Do this along the *next* line, and a membrane-free segment will fall into the sieve (and the juice into the bowl).

Cauliflower with cheese fondue sauce

You can leave the cauliflower whole or divide it into florets before steaming. The latter will take about 3 minutes over boiling salted water; the former about 20 minutes, depending on size.

1 medium cauliflower, steamed
salt and freshly ground black
 pepper
Cheese fondue sauce
7½ fl oz (225 ml) dry white
 wine
1 garlic clove, peeled and lightly
 crushed

8 oz (225 g) Gruyère cheese,
 cubed
1 level dessertspoon cornflour
½ teaspoon dry English
 mustard powder

For the sauce, heat the wine gently with the crushed garlic. In a mixing bowl, toss the cubes of cheese in the cornflour. Remove the garlic from the wine (it can be used when next making gravy, soup or stock).

Add the mustard powder, cheese and cornflour to the wine and place over a low heat, stirring gently until the cheese is fully melted and smooth. It will be very 'stringy'.

Place your cooked cauliflower in a dish and pour over the fondue sauce. If serving florets, place them on individual, warmed plates and simply pour the sauce over them. Serve on to plates using a fish slice.

Previous page: Lamb fillet with water chestnuts, orange segments and watercress, served with Baked potato circles and Cauliflower with cheese fondue sauce.

Baked potato circles

————————•————————

These are simplicity itself, but oh so good and, better still, oh so easy!

1¼ lb (550 g) potatoes, peeled   *salt and freshly ground black*
4 oz (100 g) butter, melted   *pepper*

Pre-heat the oven to gas mark 6, 400°F (200°C).

Thinly slice the potatoes into circles – for 6 people you'll need about 60 circles. Paint a large baking tray lightly with a little of the butter.

Remembering that you have to get 6 composite circles on the tray, start making the first one in a corner. Lay one slice down and then lay another 7 or 8 circles around it, overlapping, to make a neat potato circle (as if you were putting the top on a hot-pot). Repeat this 5 more times on separate parts of the tray, so that you have 6 good potato circles. Paint with the remaining melted butter and season with salt and pepper. Bake in the pre-heated oven for 15 minutes, then remove and leave to go cold. Cover.

When you wish to serve, pre-heat the oven to gas mark 4, 350°F (180°C), and bake for a further 15–20 minutes. A fish slice will transfer them easily from the baking tray to your warm dinner plates.

Simple egg custards

————————•————————

This recipe actually makes *seven* custards in ramekins 3 in (7.5 cm) in diameter and 1 in (2.5 cm) deep: one extra as a perk for the cook! Serve them with the following recipe for Sugared bread triangles.

10 fl oz (300 ml) double cream   *freshly grated nutmeg*
10 fl oz (300 ml) milk   *7 tablespoons liqueur or brandy*
3 oz (75 g) soft brown sugar   *(optional)*
6 medium free-range eggs

Pre-heat the oven to gas mark 2, 300°F (160°C).

Beat the first 5 ingredients together in a bowl. Then divide between your 7 ramekins. A tablespoon of liqueur or brandy in the base of each ramekin before filling will uplift this simple dish! Place the ramekins in a roasting tray and pour enough warm water into the tray to come half-way up the sides of the ramekins. Bake in the pre-heated oven for 40 minutes, then remove from the oven. Leave to go cold, cover with cling film and put in the fridge.

Fan-assisted ovens make the custards rise whilst cooking but they come to no harm!

Sugared bread triangles

Serve these with the egg custards above, or with the Raspberry syllabub on p. 92.

6 thin slices of white bread,
crusts removed
about 1 oz (25 g) unsalted
butter

2 oz (50 g) vanilla sugar (caster
sugar which has been stored
with a vanilla pod)
1 teaspoon powdered cinnamon
or mixed spice (optional)

Pre-heat the oven to gas mark 4, 350°F (180°C).

Very, very lightly butter the bread on both sides. Cut into 24 triangles and arrange on a baking sheet. Bake in the pre-heated oven for 15 minutes. Remove from the oven and coat generously with vanilla sugar – if you like, mix the suggested spice with the sugar before coating. Leave on kitchen paper to drain and become cold.

Previous page: Simple egg custards, accompanied by Sugared bread triangles.

SHOPPING LIST

Butcher
1 lb 2 oz (500 g) lamb fillet

Baker
bread for breadcrumbs
6 slices white bread

Grocer
2 tablespoons olive oil
9 oz (250 g) butter
6 eggs
10 fl oz (300 ml) double cream
10 fl oz (300 ml) milk
8 oz (225 g) Gruyère cheese
3 tablespoons grated Parmesan
  cheese
1 level dessertspoon cornflour
½ teaspoon dry English mustard
  powder
3 oz (75 g) soft brown sugar
2 oz (50 g) vanilla sugar
12 canned water chestnuts

Greengrocer
12 courgettes, about 4 oz (100 g)
  each
1¼ lb (550 g) potatoes
1 medium cauliflower
about 10 oz (275 g) onions
2 red peppers
3 garlic cloves
1 bunch of watercress
3 oranges

Off-licence
7½ fl oz (225 ml) dry white wine
7 tablespoons liqueur or brandy
  (optional)

Store-cupboard
salt and freshly ground black
  pepper
freshly grated nutmeg
powdered cinnamon or mixed spice

COUNTDOWN

D-DAY MINUS ONE

AM

Cook the egg custards, leave to cool, cover with cling film and store in the fridge.

PM (in the evening)

Prepare and stuff the courgettes, cover with cling film and store in the fridge.

Prepare the lamb fillet, water chestnuts, oranges and watercress. Store separately in the fridge.

Prepare and part-bake the potato circles. Leave to go cold, then cover and store in the fridge.

Prepare and cook the Sugared bread triangles. Cool and store in an air-tight box.

D-DAY

AM

1 hour before you sit down

Pre-heat the oven to gas mark 4, 350°F (180°C).

45 minutes before you sit down

Put the courgettes in the oven.

Remove the egg custards from the fridge, place the ramekins on individual plates and decorate with the Sugared bread triangles.

20 minutes before you sit down

Make the cheese sauce and leave in a bowl over simmering water.

10 minutes before you sit down

Put the plates for the starter into the oven to warm through.

Serving the starter

Start steaming the whole cauliflower. (If using florets steam at the last minute).

Put the potato circles in the oven to cook.

Put the plates for the main course into the oven to warm through.

Start to heat the oil and butter for the stir-fry.

Remove the courgettes from the oven and serve.

Serving the main course

First you have to cook it! Stir-fry the lamb and warm through the other ingredients. Portion on to individual hot plates.

Pour the sauce over the cauliflower, then portion it and the potatoes. Serve.

Serving the dessert

If you are feeling totally decadent a twirl of lightly whipped, sweetened double cream, decorated with a sprig of mint, will enhance the look.

SUMMER

·

My real summer is in the British winter, when I take off to warmer climes, usually South Africa. However, at home I can still enjoy many British summer benefits (when the weather allows me), organising picnics, barbecues, candle-lit dinners, etc.

Mother Nature has almost been over-indulgent and has given us a superabundance of foods in the summer months. Chicken and poultry are favourites, as they are incredibly versatile, light, and delicious hot or cold. Do, however, buy fresh, free-range birds. And there are no worries about what to serve as a dessert because there is such a wealth of summer fruit around.

Once again, table flowers are no problem at this time, and I usually choose a pink and green theme which goes well with most china. I like to scatter cherubs around summer lunch or dinner tables!

WINES FOR SUMMER PARTIES

The poultry dishes I've chosen are all quite gutsy and need a distinctive grape to accompany them. As a result, I have gone for wines made from a blend of the Merlot grape. The New World wine-makers blend it with their Cabernet Sauvignon: Cloudy Bay from New Zealand is a prime example and, from Australia, the Cullens, Dromana and Tim Knappstein Clare Valley.

To accompany the starters, I have settled for wines made from the Sémillon grape. Australia proudly boasts a Hill Smith and Rothbury Hunter Valley, and I adore the Hupai Mercury Bay from New Zealand.

To go with the glorious summer fruits I must admit I invariably go for a chilled glass of Vouvray from the Loire or a classical Sauternes.

Or you could serve a Pimms-like drink. Mix together in a glass jug ¼ gill (1¼ fl oz or about 30 ml) each of gin, red vermouth and orange Curaçao (or Grand Marnier). Add two pieces each of apple and cucumber, a slice of orange, some mint and a big sprig of borage. Fill up with 1 pint (600 ml) lemonade, add lots of ice, and serve in glass tankards. Or you could offer a simple iced tea.

Summer Menu One

Choux Eclairs with Cheese and Herb Pâté,
Bovril and Pineapple

•

Warm Roast Chicken Basted with
Lemon and Honey
accompanied by
Stir-fried Mangetouts
New Potatoes with French Dressing
Tomato Basil Sauce

•

Summer Fruits in Dessert Wine Aspic

———————————————•———————————————

I love giving lunch parties in
the summer, and in my usual fashion I choose recipes that
can be prepared well in advance so that I too can enjoy the
sunshine as much as everyone else.

I also occasionally like surprising my guests, and the
choux pastry starter here, when your guests see it, will make
them think you have gone bonkers. *'Chocolate éclairs!'* they'll
expostulate as they are shown to the table, but worried
brows will soon become bright smiles when they start tuck-

ing in. Choux pastry is easy provided you weigh everything out accurately and use *strong* plain flour. I like this combination of the cool sharp Cheese and herb pâté with the crisp choux and the salty savoury tang of the Bovril.

Chicken cooked this way is deliciously succulent, but you *must* choose a good free-range bird. Those poor battery birds live such an appalling and unhappy life, and produce such tasteless flesh. I think much more lobbying should be done on this aspect of egg and chicken production in this country, and much more encouragement given to the numerous small genuine poultry farmers. Seek out a supplier of fresh free-range products, and I guarantee you'll be amazed at the difference.

Salads are what everyone likes in the summer, and many of the salad basics are at their best now. You could serve a salad – see p. 104 – with the chicken if you like instead of the mangetouts, or indeed any other summer vegetable. It should be fairly simple, though, as the mingled tastes of the chicken mayonnaise and the sauce are rich.

Summer fruits are wonderful and really don't need much doing to them. However, this jelly is a delicious way of serving them – and they *look* so good. Seek out the best possible aspic (I like that from Switzerland), which is sold in individual foil packets. When using it, follow the packet instructions carefully. In fact, to be safe, if working with aspic for the first time, I would make up a mix but using *water*. If it set to my satisfaction, I would chuck that away and then substitute the wine (which should be rich and buttery).

Choux éclairs with cheese and herb pâté, Bovril and pineapple

This is rather a naughty starter dish. If you saw the television programme in which I made it, you will have heard me saying that when your guests sit down they will be simply stunned. For what they appear to be confronted by is a chocolate éclair on a slice of pineapple! Nothing could be further from the truth, because the éclair is filled with Cheese and herb pâté, and topped not with chocolate but Bovril.

5 fl oz (150 ml) cold water
2 oz (50 g) butter, broken into
 very small pieces
2½ oz (65 g) strong plain flour
a generous pinch of salt
2 medium free-range eggs,
 lightly beaten

Filling and garnish
12 oz (350 g) Cheese and herb
 pâté (see p. 209)
6 tablespoons Bovril
6 slices of fresh pineapple
little savoury salads

Place the water and butter in a saucepan and allow to melt over a very low heat. (If the heat is high, the water will evaporate a little and won't be able to take up the flour.) When melted, turn the heat up as high as possible and the mix will initially bubble and boil. At this stage, throw in the sifted strong flour and salt and, using a round-edged wooden spoon, bash the living daylights out of the mix, the back of the spoon beating against the sides of the saucepan. It is often easier to do this if you hold the spoon fairly low down the handle. The mixture looks rather unsightly.

Then, little by little, beat in your beaten eggs. Do this slowly, taking some time, and never add and beat in more egg until the flour mixture has taken up the egg already in it. The initial dull basic roux will soon develop

Previous page: White, green and pink for a summer lunch in the garden. The starter is Choux éclairs with Cheese and herb pâté, Bovril and pineapple, with a little savoury salad. I like to serve a Pimms-like drink beforehand.

quite a sheen and a lovely texture. When it comes together in a gungey ball and leaves the sides of the pan clean, it is ready.

Pre-heat the oven to gas mark 6, 400°F (200°C), and have ready a baking tray lined with good-quality greaseproof paper. (A little butter underneath will help keep the paper in place.)

Place the choux pastry mixture in a piping bag with a plain ½-in (1-cm) nozzle – use a *plastic* nozzle, not metal – and pipe 6 éclairs on to the paper, cutting them off with a knife. Leave as much space as possible between them so that they can rise and brown.

Sprinkle a little cold water on to the piped éclairs, double-check that the oven has reached the correct temperature and turn it up to gas mark 7, 425°F (220°C). Pop the baking tray with the éclairs into the oven and leave to bake for 20 minutes. Remove from the oven and leave to cool.

Make a cut in the sides of the éclairs and pipe the Cheese and herb pâté into them. Have the Bovril melting in a saucer over a pan of simmering water and simply dip the top of each éclair into this. Arrange on suitable plates on top of the pineapple slices and garnish with a few little salad items. What could be simpler!

Warm roast chicken basted with lemon and honey

A summertime lunch dish which is popular with guests at the farm as the lemon and honey baste goes so well with the fresh thyme and orange juice.

1 fresh chicken, preferably weighing about 4 lb (1.75 kg)
2 oranges, halved
4 sprigs of fresh thyme
sea salt and freshly ground black pepper
4 oz (100 g) soft butter

4 tablespoons good-quality local runny honey
1 tablespoon fresh lemon juice

To serve
shredded iceberg lettuce
Garlic oil (see p. 250)
Curry mayonnaise (see p. 250)

Wipe the chicken dry and in the ribcage put 2 of the orange halves along with 2 of the thyme sprigs. Season well with sea salt and pepper, then squeeze the remaining halves of orange over it and 'clart' on the soft butter. Put the other 2 sprigs of thyme between the thighs and breasts. Cover with foil and leave until you wish to cook.

Pre-heat the oven to gas mark 6, 400°F (200°C).

Roast the chicken in the pre-heated oven for an hour, pour off fat and juices, then turn the temperature down to gas mark 4, 350°F (180°C). Spoon on the mixed honey and lemon juice and baste every 10 minutes for another 30 minutes or so.

Remove from the oven, cover with foil and leave to settle for 15–30 minutes. Portion by cutting off the legs and dividing each in two. Turn and cut off the wings. Cut down the middle of the chicken, using a very sharp knife, then pull the breasts off the bird. Divide these in two. Don't forget about the oysters of meat underneath. Strip the carcass of all the

Warm roast chicken served with New potatoes with French dressing, Stir-fried mangetouts, and a dollop each of Curry mayonnaise and Tomato basil sauce.

meat and save the bones, etc., for making yourself a good home-made stock later (see p. 249).

The chicken can obviously be served just as it is, with all the accompaniments as in the photograph, but what I like to do is arrange it on a platter of shredded iceberg lettuce dressed lightly with Garlic oil (see p. 250), and cover the meat itself with Curry mayonnaise (see p. 250). Then you can serve individual plates of chicken and mayonnaise, with criss-crossed mangetouts, warm New potatoes with French dressing, a spoonful of Tomato basil sauce and lots of chopped chives.

Stir-fried mangetouts

This small amount of mangetouts is sufficient for six average portions, and so is relatively inexpensive.

> *4 oz (100 g) fresh mangetouts*   *1 oz (25 g) butter*
> *1 tablespoon olive oil*

Top and tail the peas and see that the strings are removed. Put in a shallow basin, cover with ice cubes and leave in the fridge until just prior to cooking them.

In a small frying-pan heat the olive oil and butter. Strain the mangetouts, pat dry, then simply stir-fry for 3 minutes. Serve at once.

New potatoes with French dressing

New potatoes are also wonderful simply boiled with a sprig of mint and then served with a little butter. They're also very good in potato salads with some cream-diluted Mayonnaise (see p. 250).

24 small unpeeled new
   potatoes, scrubbed
2 pints (1.2 litres) cold water

salt
10 fl oz (300 ml) French
   dressing (see p. 240)

Place the potatoes in a pan, cover with the water and add salt to taste. Bring to the boil. Turn heat down and simmer for 20 minutes. Drain well, then place in a serving dish. Heat the French dressing, pour over the potatoes while they are still warm. Serve warm or cool.

Tomato basil sauce

This rather cowboy method makes for a relatively smooth and terribly tasty sauce.

2 oz (50 g) soft butter
2 level teaspoons runny salt
6 oz (175 g) onions, peeled and
   finely chopped
2 lb (900 g) tomatoes, wiped
   clean and each chopped into 4
   wedges

5 fl oz (150 ml) cooking sherry
at least 20 large leaves of fresh
   basil (the quantity will vary,
   depending on how strong and
   large the leaves are!)
sugar (optional)
a little white wine (optional)

Melt the butter in a large saucepan and add the next 5 ingredients. Give a good stir with a wooden spoon, then spread a double thickness of good greaseproof paper on top. Allow to simmer away for about 1 hour until the mixture is quite thick and on the dry side. (Check every now and again, though, to see it's not sticking.)

Remove from the heat, liquidise and pass through a coarse sieve. Leave to cool.

Adjust the seasoning when you re-heat the sauce by adding sugar, salt or a little more basil liquidised in some white wine. (The sauce can actually be served hot *or* cold.)

Summer fruits in dessert wine aspic

There is no need to get frantic searching for splendid recipes with which to end a summer party as the Good Lord has provided us with such an abundance of summer fruits. Any of them can be used in this dish, preferably the smaller soft berries and fruit. For the TV programme I used blackberries, raspberries, black and red currants, blueberries and quartered strawberries. To flavour the aspic, Beaumes de Venise is ideal and Frangelico is fantastic, as are some of the very sweet wines from the New World.

Look around for some unusually shaped glasses or glass dishes to serve the fruit in. I often use reject Manhattan cocktail glasses.

If you like, serve the glasses on a small plate covered with a doily, and decorate the plate with a little spray of garden herbs and flowers.

about 1 lb 2 oz (500 g) varied
soft fruits, prepared (see above)
1 oz (25 g) soft brown sugar

1 packet good-quality aspic
powder
10 fl oz (300 ml) dessert wine
(see above)

Divide the fruits equally between 6 glasses, filling them two thirds full, and sprinkle each with a teaspoon of the sugar.

Make up the aspic powder according to the instructions on the packet, but using your chosen wine instead of water. When it is cooling and beginning to set, divide between the glasses. Leave to cool – it takes about an hour to set – then cover lightly with cling film and leave in the fridge.

Take out of the fridge when you are serving the main course and leave somewhere cool. If it is too cold when served, the flavours of the wine and of the fruit are deadened. And don't be tempted to do anything elaborate with cream; it is not necessary.

Previous page: Summer fruits – here strawberries and raspberries – in dessert wine aspic.

SHOPPING LIST

Butcher

1 × 4 lb (1.75 kg) fresh chicken

Grocer

about 1½ pints (900 ml) olive oil
3–4 tablespoons white wine vinegar
14 oz (400 g) butter
4 eggs
1 lb (450 g) cream cheese
2½ oz (65 g) strong plain flour
1 oz (25 g) soft brown sugar
½ teaspoon caster sugar
4 tablespoons runny honey
6 tablespoons Bovril
1 packet good-quality aspic powder
2 tablespoons apricot jam

Off-licence

5 fl oz (150 ml) red wine
10 fl oz (300 ml) good-quality
  dessert wine
5 fl oz (150 ml) cooking sherry

Greengrocer

24 small new potatoes
2 lb (900 g) tomatoes
10 oz (275 g) onions
15–18 garlic cloves
1 iceberg lettuce and salad
  ingredients for savoury salads
4 oz (100 g) mangetouts
1 tablespoon of fresh chervil,
  parsley and chives (or whatever
  fresh herbs are available)
4 sprigs of fresh thyme
at least 20 fresh basil leaves
1 lb 2 oz (500 g) varied soft fruits
2 oranges
6 slices of fresh pineapple
1 lemon

Store-cupboard

salt and freshly ground black
  pepper
¾ teaspoon dry English mustard
  powder
Curry essence (see p. 252)

Summer Menu Two

Gravadlax with Fanned Spiced Pear Halves

•

Boned Quail Stuffed with
Chicken Pistachio Cream
accompanied by
Curried Cubed Fried Potatoes
Broad Beans with Bacon and Walnut

•

Raspberry Syllabub

———————————•———————————

This is the sort of meal that I would like to serve on a warm summer's evening, preferably in the open air (but fairly near to the kitchen). A few garden lamps, a chiller for the white wines, and I would be in heaven. If it rained, I would set up candles all round the conservatory – the food would taste just as good!

I love gravadlax, much richer and more succulent than smoked salmon (although I'm not averse to plentiful helpings of that). Gravadlax bought in packs is so expensive (and mean in quantity) that I really cannot emphasise enough how basically easy it is to make. The sea salt crystals are more expensive but essential. During the marination of the tail fillets, the salts, sugars and spices do all the work for you, and all you have to remember is to turn the foil package over and re-weight it, morning and night. You could serve the gravadlax by itself, with some lightly buttered rye or pumpernickel bread.

Boned quail are to be seen much more often now on supermarket shelves, and I think they are a wonderful idea for an entertaining occasion. You don't have to worry about carving or portioning a larger bird, and they take such a short time to cook. The chicken pistachio cream stuffing is wonderful, but of course you could ring the changes here (substituting a cream cheese-based stuffing, for instance, or something similar). If you haven't got a food processor for the stuffing, simply halve the recipe and run it twice through your liquidiser.

The vegetables are a good combination, full of flavour, but of course you could substitute something else. I admit to both taking a little time to prepare (although still in advance), but both are well worth the effort, particularly the broad beans, by far my favourite summer vegetable.

A syllabub is simplicity itself, virtually just a flavoured whipped cream. Served in glasses with the rosy glow of the raspberry purée at the bottom, it looks very pretty, an attractive finish to your meal. The cream could be flavoured differently of course – traditionally the flavouring is sherry – and you could substitute any other summer fruit for the raspberries (strawberries or fresh apricots perhaps).

Gravadlax

The tail of the salmon should be purchased from your fishmonger for this dish. Have a bit of cheek and query why you should be paying the same amount per lb (450 g) for this cut as you would be for the more succulent, thicker, richer middle! Allow 3 days for the gravadlax to develop and then, using a very sharp, serrated knife, slice it very thinly.

1 tail end of salmon, weighing
  about 1¼ lb (550 g)
6 oz (175 g) coarse sea salt
12 oz (350 g) demerara sugar
3 tablespoons cooking brandy
6 tablespoons rosé wine
finely grated rind and juice of 2
  oranges
1 kernel preserved ginger, finely
  chopped

2 tablespoons finely chopped
  fresh dill
6 black peppercorns, bashed
  coarsely in a pestle and mortar
To serve
fanned spiced pear halves (see
  next recipe)
Mustard, dill and molasses
  mayonnaise (see p. 250)

Remove the skin and bone from the salmon, after which you should be left with approximately 1 lb (450 g) weight. You will have two strips of 'fillet' about 6–7 in (15–18 cm) long.

Lay a doubled 12-in (30-cm) square of foil on your work surface, dull side up. Combine the sea salt and demerara sugar, and spread a quarter of this out on the foil. Put one piece of the salmon down on this, so that one side is virtually coated with the 'pickling' mixture. Dribble over half of the mixed brandy and *rosé* wine. Put a third of the remaining salt/sugar mix on top and then sprinkle with half the orange rind and juice, and half the ginger, dill and peppercorns.

Take the other piece of fish and lay on a similarly sized piece of foil. Sprinkle with the remaining brandy/*rosé* mix, and orange, ginger, dill,

Previous page: Creamy yellow-peach colours for a summer dinner party. The starter is Gravadlax with Fanned spiced pear halves, served with Mustard, dill and molasses mayonnaise.

etc., and then with half the remaining salt/sugar mix. Invert this carefully, so that none of the liquid is lost, on to the other piece of fish, to make a 'sandwich'. Remove the top piece of foil so that you can sprinkle on the remaining salt/sugar mix, then tightly wrap both pieces of foil round the salmon, sealing all sides well.

Put on a tray and cover with either 2 house bricks or 2 × 2 lb (900 g) weights. (It is the firm pressing that makes the marinade mix penetrate through the flesh.) Store in the fridge and turn the foil package, re-weighting it each time, morning and night for 3 days.

Remove the fillets from the foil, scrape off the gunge and slice through thinly as for smoked salmon. Serve on individual plates with the fanned pear slices, and the mayonnaise.

*F*anned spiced pear halves

These add an interesting texture and flavour to the gravadlax dish, and when the thin slices of fish are draped over the sliced pear, it looks quite substantial and utterly irresistible. The pears are also delicious with air-dried and cured meats.

3 pears	*caster sugar*
water	*white wine vinegar*

Peel the pears, take the middle core out from each one through the base. Leave the top (stalk) end whole. Stand the pears in a very small saucepan which will securely hold them all, bottoms down, in a vertical manner.

Pour in enough water to come half-way up the pan and then pour it out and measure it. If you have used, say, 10 fl oz (300 ml) liquid, throw in 1 lb (450 g) caster sugar (in other words, 2 parts sugar to 1 part water). For each 10 fl oz (300 ml) liquid you also need 2 tablespoons white wine vinegar.

Simmer the pears in the water, sugar and vinegar mix until they are soft but still retain a slight bite. This can easily be tested by using a small sharp-pointed kitchen knife. Leave to one side and allow to cool.

To serve, cut the pears lengthwise in half, and then slice finely about two-thirds through. Fan out on the individual plates before garnishing or covering with succulent slices of the gravadlax.

Boned quail stuffed with chicken pistachio cream

Although a good friend of mine says that quail always remind her of dead budgies on her plate, don't let this put you off, because this recipe is rich, succulent and satisfying!

6 boned quail
3 oz (75 g) butter, melted
salt and freshly ground black
  pepper
6 Large-base croûtons (optional,
  see p. 248)
6 tiny sprigs of parsley

Chicken pistachio cream
6 oz (175 g) skinned chicken
  breast
1 medium free-range egg
just over 5 fl oz (150 ml)
  double cream
3 level tablespoons shelled
  pistachio nuts

For the chicken cream, cut up the chicken breast, put in your food processor and blend, gradually adding the egg and double cream. Season well with salt and pepper, then fold in the pistachio nuts.

Spoon or pipe into the boned quail, and lay on a greased baking tray. Cover and chill. When you want to cook, pre-heat the oven to gas mark 7, 425°F (220°C). Brush the melted butter over the quail and season them. Place the tray in the oven and cook the quail for 20–25 minutes. Serve hot, on the warmed croûtons if using, garnished with parsley.

Boned stuffed quail on a Large-base croûton, served with Curried cubed fried potatoes and Broad beans with bacon and walnut.

Curried cubed fried potatoes

———————————————————— • ————————————————————

These are decidedly decadent, and I always do more than I really need as guests, more often than not, eagerly accept second helpings. Remember, though, when buying curry powder to get it in *small* tins as, once opened, the flavour soon deteriorates. Personally I think time is well spent making your own Curry essence (see p. 252) which is added to the oil and butter before the potatoes.

1 lb (450 g) old potatoes, peeled   *2 oz (50 g) butter*
salt   *2 level teaspoons curry powder*
2 tablespoons olive oil

Cut the potatoes into ¼-in (5-mm) slices and then cut each slice into cubes of equal size. Put the cubes in a saucepan of cold salted water, bring to the boil and cook for 2 minutes. Drain and refresh under cold water. Dry well on kitchen paper.

    In a frying-pan heat the oil and butter and then add the potato cubes. Sprinkle on the curry powder and cook until fairly crisp. This should take about 15 minutes.

Broad beans with bacon and walnut

———————————————————— • ————————————————————

Broad beans as fresh as a daisy are my very favourite vegetable and I regret so much that the season is relatively short. I know the frozen kind are readily available, but for me they simply are not the same, no matter what you do to them, so you should pass them by when shopping in the supermarket.

    It may be a chore doing them the way I like – and which I specify opposite – but as the occasion arises only about eight times a year I do not begrudge a single minute!

3 lb (1.3 kg) broad bean pods
salt
4 oz (100 g) smoked bacon,
   rinded and diced

1 tablespoon walnut oil
1 oz (25 g) shelled walnuts,
   coarsely chopped

Remove the beans from their pods and then either steam over or simmer in boiling salted water until just getting soft (about 2–4 minutes' boiling or steaming, but it all depends on the age of the beans). Transfer to a sieve and refresh under cold running water. Then, if you have the patience, sit down and painstakingly pop each bright green inner bean out of the greyish shell. When cold, cover and put to one side.

The bacon could also be cooked in the oil in advance until crisp. Leave in the pan, covered.

When you wish to serve, simply put the beans in the pan with the bacon and re–heat gently for about 10 minutes, perhaps while everyone is eating their starter. Just before serving, scatter the walnuts over the dish.

Raspberry syllabub

If you have an old-fashioned gill measure, the 7½ fl oz (225 ml) of booze is easy to measure. Use a good, but not frightfully expensive, dessert wine or, if you can get it, the Italian Frangelico.

2 lemons	**Raspberry purée**
1 orange	*4 oz (100 g) fresh raspberries*
7½ fl oz (225 ml) booze of	*25 g (1 oz) icing sugar*
your choice (see above)	**Garnish**
15 fl oz (450 ml) double cream	*a few fresh raspberries*
2 oz (50 g) soft brown sugar	*6 sprigs of fresh mint*
	Sugared bread triangles
	(see p. 56)

Wipe the lemons and orange clean with a damp cloth and dry. Finely grate the rind from them, and then cut them in half and squeeze out the juice. Transfer the rind and juice to a bowl and mix in the booze. Cover and leave in the fridge for at least 4 hours.

Meanwhile, mash the raspberries for the purée with the icing sugar, using a silver fork, to make a gungey mix. Pass through a sieve. Have to hand the 6 glasses you have selected to serve this pud in and divide the raspberry gunge between them.

In your mixer put the double cream and soft brown sugar and beat until the mixture starts to become stiff. Then, tablespoon by tablespoon, add the booze mix, still beating. This takes time and patience, but the cream *will* take up all the liquid.

Spoon this wonderfully flavoured cream on top of the raspberry purée in the glasses, then cover each glass with cling film. Put in the fridge for up to 6 hours. Take out of the fridge about 30 minutes before serving and garnish with fresh raspberries, mint and Sugared bread triangles.

Previous page: Raspberry syllabub, garnished with mint, and accompanied by Sugared bread triangles.

SHOPPING LIST

Fishmonger
1 tail end of salmon, about 1¼ lb
  (550 g)

Butcher
6 boned quail
6 oz (175 g) chicken breast
4 oz (100 g) smoked bacon

Baker
bread for croûtons and bread
  triangles

Grocer
11 fl oz (325 ml) olive oil
1 tablespoon walnut oil
at least 2 fl oz (50 ml) white wine
  vinegar
5 oz (150 g) butter
3 eggs
1 pint (600 ml) double cream
12 oz (350 g) demerara sugar
1 lb 2 oz (500 g) caster sugar
1 oz (25 g) icing sugar
2 oz (50 g) soft brown sugar
1 tablespoon molasses or dark
  treacle
6 oz (175 g) coarse sea salt
1 kernel preserved ginger
2 tablespoons Dijon mustard
2 teaspoons curry powder

Greengrocer
1 lb (450 g) old potatoes
3 lb (1.3 kg) broad beans
4 tablespoons chopped fresh dill
6 sprigs of fresh mint
3 tablespoons shelled pistachio nuts
1 oz (25 g) shelled walnuts
3 pears
3 oranges
2 lemons
about 5 oz (150 g) fresh raspberries

Off-licence
3 tablespoons cooking brandy
6 tablespoons *rosé* wine
7½ fl oz (225 ml) dessert wine or
  Frangelico

Store-cupboard
salt and freshly ground black
  pepper
6 black peppercorns
¼ teaspoon dry English mustard
  powder

COUNTDOWN

D-DAY MINUS THREE

Prepare the gravadlax, remembering to turn it every morning and evening until your party day.

D-DAY MINUS ONE

Bake the croûtons if using (see p. 248), cool and store.

Prepare the quail stuffing, cover with cling film and store in the fridge.

Prepare the pears and Mayonnaise, cover and store in the fridge.

Prepare the booze mixture and raspberry purée for the syllabub. Store separately in the fridge.

Prepare and cook the Sugared bread triangles (see p. 56). Cool and store in an airtight box.

D-DAY

AM

Stuff the quail, cover and chill.

Prepare the potatoes, boil, drain and refresh. Dry well and keep covered.

Pod and cook the beans, then skin if you like. Cover and keep to one side.

Cook the bacon in the oil, cover and leave.

PM

Divide the raspberry purée between the glasses for the dessert; whip the syllabub and spoon on top of the purée. Cover and put in the fridge.

Slice the gravadlax and the pears, and arrange on the plates. Cover with cling film and leave in a cool place.

30 minutes before you sit down

Pre-heat the oven to gas mark 7, 425°F (220°C).

5 minutes before you sit down

Put the quail into the oven to cook.

Serving the starter

Start frying the potato cubes over a gentle heat.

Re-heat the beans and bacon in the bacon pan.

Put the plates for the main course, and the croûtons (if using), into the oven to warm through.

Serve the starter, each plate garnished with a blob of Mayonnaise.

Serving the main course

Turn up the heat under the potato cubes and fry until crisp.

Remove the quail from the oven and place on the croûtons (if using) on individual hot plates. Divide the potato cubes and broad beans (sprinkle with the walnuts) between the plates and serve.

Take the dessert out of the fridge.

Serving the dessert

Garnish the syllabubs and serve.

Summer Menu Three

Prawn and Smoked Salmon Cheese Slice

•

Breast of Chicken in Puff Pastry
accompanied by
Calvados Apple Purée
Seasonal Salad

•

Gooseberry Cake with Orange custard

One of my favourite entertaining occasions in the summer is a glamorous picnic. None of your plastic plates and spoons for me – I go the whole hog. I take my carefully wrapped china plates (not the Meissen, I hasten to add, but perhaps a set bought from a junk shop or car boot sale), good cutlery and proper glasses. I can't abide drinking wine out of paper cups, but you can now buy some very good-looking plastic 'glasses' (from Italy, I think). I also take with me ground sheets, rugs, cushions, collapsible chairs – I like to be *comfortable* when I'm having a good time.

The food itself is all packed carefully into large wicker

baskets (I never seem to be able to fit things into actual picnic hampers), utilising foil, cling film, rigid boxes and containers of all kinds, and screw-top jars for the sauces, dressings, etc. None of the recipes in this menu would be too difficult to transport – but it's always easiest if you have a car! I'm actually not averse to picnicking at the bottom of the garden (it saves all that packing, unpacking and ultimate packing-up of the dirties and empties).

There are actually many other recipes throughout the book which could be taken on a picnic. Soup is not an impossibility if the day is less than tropical; take in a Thermos flask and serve in mugs with good bread (see p. 224). Many pastry dishes – especially the tiny quiches on p. 232 – travel well (so long as they are packed properly), and the dessert could be meringues, ice cream (take in a cooler bag), a farmhouse pie, egg custards or – the *easiest* – fresh fruit. The gooseberry cake is delicious, though, and only marginally less so when served cold.

If you wanted, you could change the stuffing of the chicken breast – the two old favourites, Cheese and herb and Mushroom pâtés (see pp. 209 and 204), could be used instead of the peanut butter. The chicken could have been marinating for 24 hours or so in some seasoned Greek yoghurt before drying, stuffing and wrapping in pastry (this makes it taste even more succulent). You can choose, instead of the mixed salad guidelines, one of the salads in the Vegetarian Buffet chapter (p. 228) – but as the chicken is so rich and filling, the simpler the salad, the better.

Prawn and smoked salmon cheese slice

This savoury cheese 'cake' can be made the day before your party and chilled. Do remember, though, to take it out of the fridge in good time so that it can be served at room temperature. It can serve from six to twelve depending on how mean or generous your slices are!

Base
8 oz (225 g) digestive biscuits
1 teaspoon ground coriander
finely grated rind of 1 lemon
2 oz (50 g) butter, melted
Filling
½ oz (15 g) powdered gelatine
juice of 1 lemon made up to 5
   tablespoons with dry white
   wine

8 oz (225 g) good cream cheese
4 level tablespoons Mayonnaise
   (see p. 250)
1 tablespoon horseradish cream
5 fl oz (150 ml) double cream
5 oz (150 g) Greek yoghurt
8 oz (225 g) cooked prawns,
   peeled and roughly chopped
4 oz (100 g) smoked salmon,
   diced

Pre-heat the oven to gas mark 4, 350°F (180°C). Have ready an 8-in (20-cm) spring-sided sponge tin which you have fully lined with good-quality greaseproof paper.

For the base, crush the biscuits one by one in a liquidiser, or simply put them in a large plastic bag and bash with a rolling pin to form fine crumbs. Mix with the coriander, lemon rind and melted butter. Spread the biscuit mix into the tin and bake in the pre-heated oven for 20 minutes. Remove and leave to go quite cold.

For the filling, add the gelatine to the 5 tablespoons of lemon juice and white wine and leave to one side.

In a bowl beat the cream cheese, Mayonnaise, horseradish, double cream and yoghurt together until thick. Using a long-handled spoon, carefully fold in the prawns and smoked salmon.

Previous page: The ingredients of a perfect picnic – a Prawn and smoked salmon cheese slice, a Breast of chicken in puff pastry, and a Gooseberry cake.

Put the saucepan of gelatine over the lowest possible heat and very gently bring round. Pour on to the fish mix through a fine, warmed metal sieve and combine well. Pour on to the biscuit base and leave to set in the fridge – it will need about 3 hours. Take out of the fridge about 30 minutes before serving and remove from the tin. Serve cut into wedges.

Breast of chicken in puff pastry

I must immediately say that this is a right 'parp' to do – time-consuming, tricky, annoying *but* worth every single moment spent. Not only do the flavours excite, but the sheer look of the finished dish invites favourable comments from your guests. The peanut butter is good for you, the chicken is soft and succulent, and the pastry is filling and – yes, I suppose – fattening!

At the end of each season at Miller Howe we have to host a group of the loveliest 'millionaires' who, whilst demanding and knowing *exactly* what they want, just simply could not be nicer people to look after – and we have been looking after them these last fourteen years! Each Friday the men go on very adventurous difficult walks with two professional guides while I take the – dare I say, more sane – others on a walk that Ozzie and I enjoy. Last year, in our packed lunch lockers, this was the main dish accompanied by a round of wine-jellied vegetables and a home-made bap filled with delicious local cheese and home-made chutney.

Ozzie thoroughly enjoyed the breast of chicken in puff pastry but totally refused to have anything to do with the jellied vegetables!

1 lb (450 g) Puff pastry
(see p. 245)
6 boned chicken breasts
6 dessertspoons peanut butter
(smooth or chunky)

salt and freshly ground black
pepper
1 free-range egg, beaten

Be sure the pastry is at room temperature, then divide it into 6 equal pieces. Roll out each piece until it is quite thin and cut into strips that are just over ¼ in (5 mm) wide.

Lay the chicken breasts on the work surface and insert 1 dessertspoon peanut butter between each fillet and breast of the chicken. Liberally season each breast with salt and pepper.

Painstakingly start winding the strips of puff pastry round each chicken breast, starting at one end and overlapping the strips slightly. Always have the join on the base part. Put the prepared chicken breasts on a baking tray, cover and chill. This can be done the evening before a lunch; the morning before a dinner.

When you want to cook, pre-heat the oven to gas mark 7, 425°F (220°C). The accuracy of the temperature is most important.

Brush the beaten egg over the pastry and bake in the pre-heated oven for exactly 30 minutes. Remove from the oven and serve hot; if left to go cold, the chicken can be wrapped in cling film and taken on a picnic.

Calvados apple purée

———————•———————

This is basically a simple apple purée or sauce – useful in itself for many purposes – with some sweetening and Calvados added. It complements the chicken beautifully, but can also be served as a pudding sauce, or as an apple filling for meringues or pavlovas (see pp. 126 and 142), or with something like pancakes.

1½ oz (40 g) unsalted butter
2 lb (900 g) Granny Smith
 apples, peeled, cored and thinly
 sliced

½ teaspoon powdered cinnamon
2 level tablespoons of soft
 brown sugar
about 2 tablespoons Calvados
 (or to taste)

Breast of chicken in puff pastry, garnished with a little savoury salad.

Pre-heat the oven to gas mark 5, 375°F (190°C). Use ½ oz (15 g) of the butter to grease a suitable flameproof casserole.

Mix the apple slices with the cinnamon, brown sugar and remaining butter and place in the casserole. Bake in the pre-heated oven for 40 minutes. Stir every now and then with a wooden spoon.

When the apples are soft, bring out of the oven and place the casserole over high heat. Heat some Calvados (as little or as much as you like) and flame over the apples. Leave to cool.

Pass the apples through a plastic sieve. Serve warm (heat carefully in a bowl over simmering water) or cold.

Seasonal salad

I prefer to arrange this in small individual bowls or plates, which I think look better, but of course you can make one large salad in a big salad bowl or dish.

It's pointless really to give a recipe as so much depends on what you have available at this time of year and where you live. Perhaps it's a better idea to give you a few alternatives, without a formal recipe structure. Think of a salad as a flower arrangement: you want colour and form, and the basic structural ingredients go in first followed by the decorative or filling-in elements.

Most of the preparation can be done in advance, and then bits brought together not too long before the party. If you want to dress the salads (see French dressing on p. 240), do so at the *very last* moment.

First layer
Using an individual small bowl or a dish, rub first with the tasty oil of your choice – olive or a nut oil. Then rub with a peeled and halved clove of garlic. Grind on some black pepper (or coriander seeds; I always have some in a pepper mill) and scatter on some finely chopped fresh herbs.

Second layer
Arrange in the bowl some basic salad leaves. The choice nowadays is

amazing – round, Cos, Webb's and iceberg lettuce, frisée, endive, etc. Have some of the prettier leaves – chicory or radicchio, say – sticking out in a star shape at the sides. Rocket, sorrel or small spinach leaves could also be used.

Third layer

You could now put a blob of Cheese and herb pâté (see p. 209) in to hold some of the more decorative items in place – slices of apple marinated in lime juice, lightly cooked and cooled French beans, slices of avocado marinated in French dressing, cooked asparagus tips, or tiny raw or blanched broccoli or cauliflower florets.

Fourth layer

In between these artistically arranged slices and shapes, you could pop sautéed button mushrooms, orange segments, cooked quails' eggs, fresh cherries, small chunks of cheese, cold meat or chicken chunks, cucumber wedges, carrot shreds or cherry tomatoes.

Fifth layer

Now you can scatter on some toasted pine kernels, sesame, sunflower or pumpkin seeds, some tiny baked or fried croûtons, some diced red, green or yellow pepper, or some finely grated orange or lemon rind. Tuck tiny sprigs of herbs in here and there.

Gooseberry cake

———————•———————

This is a deliciously soft and flavourful, gooseberry-packed sponge with a sort of *streusel* topping (to which you could add a little powdered mixed spice if you like). Serve it accompanied by Greek yoghurt, *crème fraîche*, *fromage frais* or clotted cream. If to be served at home, abandon the cream and serve it with the Orange custard on the next page. You could also serve it for afternoon tea.

*1 lb (450 g) fresh gooseberries,
  topped and tailed*
Sponge
4 oz (100 g) unsalted butter
4 oz (100 g) caster sugar
2 free-range eggs, lightly beaten
4 oz (100 g) self-raising flour

Crumble topping
4 oz (100 g) self-raising flour
2 oz (50 g) unsalted butter
3 oz (75 g) soft brown sugar

Pre-heat the oven to gas mark 4, 350°F (180°C), and line a 9-in (23-cm) spring-clip cake tin with good-quality greaseproof paper.

Make sure the gooseberries are clean and dry.

For the sponge, cream the butter and sugar together until light and fluffy. Gradually add the beaten eggs, beating all the time. Finally fold in the flour. Using a spatula, carefully spread evenly into the lined tin and place the gooseberries on top.

Working quickly, rub the topping flour and butter together, then add the sugar. Sprinkle over the top of the gooseberries in the tin and place immediately in the pre-heated oven. Bake for 1¼ hours. Remove from the oven, then leave to cool a little in the tin before taking out.

A wedge of Gooseberry cake, served with some whipped cream.

Orange custard

If you prefer a plain old-fashioned custard, just leave out the orange rind, and of course you don't need to add the brandy!

Makes 1 pint (600 ml)
6 free-range egg yolks
2 tablespoons caster sugar
2 level teaspoons cornflour

2 tablespoons cooking brandy
finely grated rind of 3 oranges
10 fl oz (300 ml) double cream
10 fl oz (300 ml) single cream

Place the first 5 ingredients in a large bowl and beat them together until smooth.

In a large thick saucepan, mix the 2 creams and bring to the boil. Do this carefully, as cream tends to boil over easily!

Pour the cream on to the other ingredients in the bowl, beat well together, then return to the saucepan over a reduced heat. Stir constantly, using a wooden spoon, until the custard starts to thicken. It is ready when it coats the back of the spoon.

This can be made in the morning, covered with butter paper and set aside. Re-heat in a bowl over a pan of simmering water.

SHOPPING LIST

Fishmonger
8 oz (225 g) cooked prawns
4 oz (100 g) smoked salmon

Butcher
6 boned chicken breasts

Grocer
10 fl oz (300 ml) olive oil
2 tablespoons white wine vinegar
10 oz (275 g) butter
8 oz (225 g) good cream cheese
5 fl oz (150 ml) double cream
5 oz (150 g) Greek yoghurt
10 fl oz (300 ml) cream, *crème fraîche*, *fromage frais* or Greek yoghurt (for the dessert if liked) or custard ingredients (see opposite)
8 oz (225 g) margarine
8 oz (225 g) shortening or white lard
5 eggs
6 dessertspoons peanut butter
1 lb (450 g) strong plain flour
8 oz (225 g) self-raising flour
4¼ oz (110 g) caster sugar
2 tablespoons soft brown sugar
3 oz (75 g) soft brown sugar
1 tablespoon horseradish cream
8 oz (225 g) digestive biscuits
½ oz (15 g) powdered gelatine
seeds and nuts for the salad if needed

Greengrocer
salad ingredients (whatever is best and available, but to include leaves, some vegetables, some fruit and fresh herbs)
2 lb (900 g) Granny Smith apples
1 lb (450 g) gooseberries
2 lemons

Off-licence
dry white wine
about 2 tablespoons Calvados

Store-cupboard
salt and freshly ground black pepper
1 teaspoon ground coriander
¼ teaspoon dry English mustard powder
½ teaspoon powdered cinnamon

AUTUMN

I love autumn because there is still so much fresh produce available – furred and feathered game, for instance, and the wonderful British apples, plums, pears and blackberries.

However, I have chosen fish as my main autumn theme; it is quite good now and not too expensive. Seek out a fishmonger who specialises in fresh fish. Frozen fish is a totally different kettle of fish (excuse the pun). The soups are all cheap and cheerful and, having mastered the basic vegetable soup recipe, you can ring the changes by using any 2 lb (900 g) vegetable mixture. The desserts are easy too, and can be useful all year round.

Blue is the colour I chose for my autumn TV table setting – place mats, candles and china. The flowers were arranged in a chipped tureen (but no one can see!), and the special feature was my tiny individual cruet sets, six pounds for the lot!

WINES FOR AUTUMN PARTIES

With fish, I tend to go for a wine made from the Sauvignon Blanc grape. I was first introduced to the French version in the late sixties by my wonderful friend Margaret Costa and, although one seldom tastes that same quality these days in French wines, the wine-makers down under have it 'off to a T'!

The one that comes out top of my list has to be the Cloudy Bay; this is hard to come by, but be diligent and try to track a bottle down. Two other superb ones come from Montana and Redwood Valley. At the cheaper end of the market (and a very good product) is La Bri Sauvage de la Bri Blanc Fumé from the sunny Cape, coming in at about half the price of the Aussies.

Seek out a supermarket *rosé* and serve this well chilled before the dinner, and to go with the soups try a medium Madeira. End the meals with a bottle of inexpensive sparkling white wine – the Nederburg Cuvée Brut NV is ideal. We use it as the basis for Buck's Fizz at the hotel, laced with fresh orange juice, when guests come down for breakfast.

Autumn Menu One

Celeriac and Apple Soup

•

Halibut Steak with Yoghurt and
Toasted Sesame Seeds
accompanied by
Stir-fried Sprouts with Bacon
Peppered Turnips and Carrots
Purée of Garlic Potatoes

•

Meringue Nests with Blackberries

———————————————— • ————————————————

*A*pproximately 98 per cent of this menu can be prepared at least a day in advance – and I dare say not many of you have experienced *that* before! And each of the recipes involved is so easy to prepare: practically foolproof.

My basic cream of vegetable soup recipe has, I'm afraid, been brought out yet again, but when you're entertaining you want to be confident, and this is so easy to do, whatever combination of vegetables you choose.

One of the things to watch with the soup is the onions;

when cooking them off, do so carefully as in no way do you want them to 'catch'. Cover the vegetables well with the greaseproof paper too; you'll be surprised how much liquid they make at the end of their simmering time.

Nothing could be simpler than the fish dish, and the textures of fish, creamy yoghurt and crisp sesame seeds are really interesting. You could use turbot or cod instead of the halibut.

The vegetables are so simple, but you could vary them or their method of cooking. (And I do urge you to make the Garlic oil used in the mashed potatoes; it adds such a fillip to so many dishes – see p. 250.)

Meringues are *not* difficult to make, despite what many people think, and they go wrong only if, say, the temperature of the oven is not correct. Perhaps now is the time to invest in an oven thermometer, one that will sit on the shelf of the oven on which you are actually going to cook the meringues; this will tell you the temperature absolutely accurately. And the egg whites can be too young – or simply not very good. If I had time to spare, I firmly believe I would form the Really Fresh Free-Range Farm Eggs Society; farm eggs come from much happier hens which are allowed to run about pecking all sorts of natural goodies and thus produce a much tastier product.

Store the meringues carefully, preferably in a rigid container. This is particularly important if you're going to freeze them, as some clot could come along and chuck a leg of lamb in on top of them.

Celeriac and apple soup

This quantity of soup will give you sufficient for six generous portions (or twelve meaner ones) because, if you are going to the trouble of making your own stock, dirtying two saucepans and the liquidiser, you want some left over that you can freeze. (Serve this for a simple supper dish, possibly with some of the bread mentioned on p. 224.)

8 oz (225 g) onions	1½ pints (900 ml) Home-made
1 lb (450 g) celeriac	stock (see p. 249)
1 lb (450 g) British apples	salt and freshly ground black
(cooking or dessert)	pepper
4 oz (100 g) butter	croûtons (see p. 248) and
5 fl oz (150 ml) inexpensive	chives, mint or parsley to
cooking sherry	garnish

First prepare the onions, celeriac and apples. To chop an onion finely, you must have a smallish, very sharp knife. (I hate a food processor for this, as I seem to get enormous lumps among gungey sludge.) Take off the sprouting end of the onion and remove the skin (ideal for the stockpot), but leave the onion *whole* with the root firmly intact. Cut *through* the middle of the root and onion, so that you have 2 sections. Lay the first section flat with the root end held by your non-working hand and, slowly but surely, cut horizontal slices two thirds of the way through, never going through the root. Then, holding the half firmly down on your work surface, make vertical cuts towards the root – once again not disturbing the root. At this stage you should be able to hold the half quite firmly up and above the work surface. Do the same with the other half. Then simply slice across the onion halves, allowing small squares of onion to fall away. A relatively simple task, once mastered.

Top, tail and peel the celeriac and cut into small dice. Wipe the apples

Previous page: A warming starter for a simple autumn supper – Celeriac and apple soup, garnished with croûtons and herbs.

with a damp cloth and then quarter them and cut into pieces about the same size as the celeriac. Leave the skin and core intact as both provide extra flavour eventually.

Melt the butter in quite a large saucepan (the vegetables, although expertly prepared, are quite large in volume). Put the onions into the pan of simmering butter and cook for a few minutes. When golden in colour, add the prepared celeriac and apples along with the sherry. Cover quite tightly with a damp double thickness of good-quality greaseproof paper and leave to simmer *slowly* for about 40–50 minutes. Do look occasionally to make sure they are not catching.

It is no use whatsoever going to all this trouble and then deciding to take a shortcut and use a bought stock cube. Heaven forbid, reader! Use some good Home-made stock (see p. 249), and add it, strained, to the pan of sweated veg. Stir well so that, when you put this into your liquidiser, you have equal parts of stock and cooked vegetables. The liquidiser should be only three quarters full. Put on the lid securely and then, holding a tea towel firmly over this, turn your liquidiser on to high speed. You will have to do at least two batches to blend the entire panful.

The next important step is to sieve the soup. The easiest way to do so is to put your (preferably) metal sieve over a bowl and use a soup ladle to force the mixture through. When all is through and it is cold, cover with cling film and put in the fridge.

You might well be wondering why there has been neither salt nor pepper used so far, but it is only when you come to re-heat a home-made soup that you get to know how the vegetables have 'come together'. Then, by using your own personal tastebuds, you can decide what to use, remembering that sugar counteracts a salty-bitter flavour, and salt and freshly ground pepper counteract a sweet flavour. You and only you will have to make this decision on the evening of your dinner party.

The soup takes about 20 minutes to re-heat to serving point. Pour into the heated bowls and sprinkle with warmed croûtons and fresh herbs.

Halibut steak with yoghurt and toasted sesame seeds

Halibut is a firm fish and a firm favourite of mine. It is the largest flat fish found in northern waters, and can weigh up to 300 lb (136 kg) and attain a length of 10 feet (3 m). That is the exception rather than the rule, however!

Toast the sesame seeds while you are cooking the meringues. Spread out on a tray and toast for 45 minutes at gas mark 3, 325°F (160°C).

6 × 6 oz (175 g) pieces of boned and skinned halibut
butter for greasing
sea salt and freshly ground black pepper
10 heaped tablespoons Greek yoghurt (just under 1 pint/ 600 ml)

10 heaped tablespoons sesame seeds (about 6 oz/175 g), toasted (see above)
6 sprigs of fresh mint

Find a roasting tray or heatproof dish that will take your 6 pieces of fish comfortably without having oceans of free space round the edges, and butter it lightly. Lay the pieces of fish flat in the tray or dish and coat fairly generously with freshly ground sea salt and pepper. Spread the cream-like yoghurt over each piece, cover with cling film and leave in the fridge overnight.

Pre-heat the oven to gas mark 4, 350°F (180°C).

Put the fish into the pre-heated oven and bake for 15 minutes. Remove from the oven, and coat the fish with the toasted sesame seeds. Finally, 'flash' under an extremely hot grill to produce a sort of treacle-toffee topping with soft, succulent, flaky fish underneath. Garnish with a sprig of mint. Quite scrumptious.

Halibut steak with yoghurt and toasted sesame seeds, accompanied by Stir-fried sprouts with bacon, Peppered turnips and carrots, and Purée of garlic potatoes.

Meringue nests with blackberries

If you are fortunate enough to be able to go blackberrying at this time of year, the ones found in the hedgerows of country lanes (preferably where large diesel lorries do not rumble through frequently!) are so much sweeter and succulent than the commercially produced ones. Served with toasted flaked almonds and possibly the last sprig of mint from your garden, these blackberry meringues look quite stunning and are so simple to prepare.

This recipe will give you sufficient for six round meringue nests *exactly*, but as they freeze or store extremely well (in plastic bags in airtight containers), the mixture could be doubled.

3 oz (75 g) old and cold free-range egg whites	**Filling**
	6 dessertspoons flaked almonds
3 oz (75 g) soft brown sugar	*10 fl oz (300 ml) double cream*
3 oz (75 g) caster sugar	*a little caster sugar*
	48 blackberries
	6 sprigs of mint

Line a flat baking tray with some good-quality greaseproof paper – this will stick to your tray better if the base is lightly buttered – and have to hand a plastic star nozzle and piping bag. (If you don't possess the normal flat baking tray, use a roasting tray, but *upside down*, so that the heat can circulate evenly all round the piped meringues.)

Pre-heat the oven to gas mark 3, 325°F (160°C).

An egg should weigh, out of the shell, 2 oz (50 g), but even the Lord in all His wisdom can't get Clara to guarantee this absolutely! So first your egg whites should be *weighed*, and for meringues nice and cold. You should use a glass or stainless-steel bowl (some plastic bowls, even in the cleanest of kitchens, seem to build up a slight layer of grease) and either an electric mixer or a hand beater.

Meringue nests with blackberries.

Having weighed the egg whites, put them into your spotlessly clean cold bowl (any sign of grease or yolk and your results will be lamentable). Start to beat and they should double in volume before you add even a grain of sugar.

Although white sugar is traditional, to make for a more autumnal appearance I mix caster sugar with soft brown (both sifted together first to make sure there are no lumps whatsoever). Add this, spoonful by spoonful, quite slowly. If you throw in a great dollop of sugar, the poor mix will lose some of its volume. Take your time – it will be well spent. (At least you won't be doing this task by hand as my Nan used to have to do!)

When you have added all the sugar quite slowly (over a period of, say, 10–12 minutes), your mixture should be very stiff. If it isn't, you've had it; your dish must have been greasy or you added the sugar too quickly.

Gently spoon the mix into your piping bag and then, holding the top of the bag with your working hand, put your thumb on the nearside of the bag with fourth finger behind and ease the mix from the top down into the bag (constantly examining the nozzle end to make sure that it doesn't splurt out). When ready, firmly secure the thumb and fourth finger of your working hand at the top of the mix, the empty part of the bag twisted, and then very gently pipe out a Catherine-wheel circle on to the paper-lined tray. Pipe round again to build up a rim for a bird's nest effect, finishing each nest with a flourish and a twirl. (A little patience and practice makes perfect.)

Place the tray of nests into the pre-heated oven and cook for 1 hour. Toast the almonds (and sesame seeds for the fish recipe) at the same time, but watch the almonds as they will brown quite quickly. Remove the nests from the oven and leave to become cold.

To fill the nests, whip the cream to soft peaks with caster sugar to taste. Spoon or pipe into each nest and top with blackberries, toasted flaked almonds and a sprig of mint.

SHOPPING LIST

Fishmonger
6 × 6 oz (175 g) pieces of boned
  and skinned halibut

Butcher
4 oz (100 g) smoked bacon

Baker
bread for croûtons

Grocer
olive oil (for Garlic oil)
2 tablespoons walnut oil
6½ oz (190 g) butter
3–4 medium eggs
10 fl oz (300 ml) double cream
1 pint (600 ml) Greek yoghurt
4 oz (100 g) caster sugar
3 oz (75 g) soft brown sugar
6 dessertspoons flaked almonds
6 oz (175 g) sesame seeds

Greengrocer
1 lb (450 g) celeriac
1 lb (450 g) Brussels sprouts
12 oz (350 g) turnips (or swede)
12 oz (350 g) carrots
1 lb (450 g) old potatoes
8 oz (225 g) onions
at least 1 bulb garlic (for Garlic oil)
chives, mint or parsley, plus 12
  sprigs of mint
1 lb (450 g) apples (cooking or
  dessert)
48 blackberries

Off-licence
5 fl oz (150 ml) cooking sherry

Store-cupboard
1½ pints (900 ml) Home-made
  stock (see p. 249)
sea salt and freshly ground black
  pepper

COUNTDOWN

D-DAY MINUS ONE

Make the Celeriac and apple soup. (The stock could have been made weeks in advance and frozen.) When cold, cover and put in the fridge.
Make the croûtons (see p. 248). Drain, cool and store in an airtight jar.
Make the meringues (or you could do this several days before). When cold, store carefully.
Toast the sesame seeds for the fish and the almonds for the meringues at the same time as baking the meringues. Cool, and store.
Part-cook the Brussels sprouts, cool, cover and store in the fridge.
Fry the chopped bacon in the oil until crisp, then cool and cover, leaving in the frying-pan.
Place the halibut in the yoghurt, cover with cling film, and leave to marinate in the fridge overnight.
You see – the majority is already done!

D-DAY

AM

Prepare and cook the Peppered turnips and carrots and the Purée of garlic potatoes. (You can have made the Garlic oil 3 weeks before!) Cool, place in separate bowls, cover with cling film and store in the fridge.
Prepare the blackberries, and put the cream in a bowl ready for whipping. Store both in the fridge.

PM

45 minutes before you sit down

Whip the double cream and divide between the meringue nests. Decorate with blackberries, almonds and mint. Cover loosely with foil, so as not to crush them, and leave somewhere cool.

20 minutes before you sit down

Pre-heat the oven to gas mark 4, 350°F (180°C). Put the soup bowls in the bottom of the oven to warm through, along with the croûtons.
Start heating the soup through gently on top of the stove.
Put two pans of warm water (to hold the bowls of veg) on top of the stove and start to heat.

10 minutes before you sit down

Put the Brussels sprouts into the bacon frying-pan, ready for re-heating.

Start re-heating the bowls of veg over the pans of water.

Pre-heat the grill.

Serving the soup

Put the fish into the oven, as well as the main-course plates.

Start gently re-heating the Brussels sprouts and bacon.

Pour the soup into the warmed bowls, sprinkle with croûtons and herbs and serve.

Serving the main course

Remove the fish from the oven, coat with sesame seeds and flash under the grill.

Portion everything on to the warm plates and serve.

Serving the dessert

Remove the foil, transfer the filled nests on to individual plates, and serve.

Autumn Menu Two

Haddock, Carrot and Orange Chowder
with Spinach Nutmeg Purée and Croûtons

•

Trellis of Sole and Salmon
accompanied by
Carrot Circles in Elderflower Syrup
Peas with Lettuce and Mint
Boiled Potatoes with Mint

•

Pear Cream Pavlova

———————————— • ————————————

*T*his could make a delightful lunch party – the soup is warming, and the sole is a delight to look at and to eat, as is the pavlova overflowing with cream and those delicious seasonal pears. Virtually everything can be done the day before, so it means a fairly unfraught morning before your guests arrive.

Fish, as I've said, are good in the autumn, and smoked haddock is a favourite of mine. Do be sure, though, to buy properly smoked haddock. Those fish which are a bright orange hue have been dyed; the good ones are much more subtle in colour and flavour. And do make absolutely sure that you have removed every single bone from the smoked haddock, or someone could choke. The chowder has a wonderful flavour, and you could of course garnish it much more simply – with just some croûtons and chopped fresh parsley. The spinach is good, though, adding colour as well as texture.

You might well curse me when you start to make the main-course fish dish, because it is so fiddly. But once the 'weaving' has been done, the rest is simple. And I guarantee that you'll be remembered for this dish alone: it's so pretty and tastes so good. The reduction of the cream for the sauce has to be done at the last minute, which is rather a shame, and you must watch it very carefully. Cream has the habit of coming very suddenly to the boil, rising to the top of the pan and spilling all over, making the sort of mess on your hob that you don't want when you've got guests in the house. Put the cream in a large *wide* pan, and put only *half* the pan over the low heat; both these precautions should help to avoid accidents.

As with the meringues in Autumn Menu One, a reliable oven temperature is vital for the pavlova, as is good-quality greaseproof paper. The pavlova can have been made well in advance – frozen even. Store in cupboard or freezer in an old round toffee tin, using the lid as a base; this prevents breakage, for meringue of all kinds is very fragile.

I must admit to the fact that this menu is not for the slimmer – there's rather a lot of cream . . .

Pre-heat the oven to gas mark 1, 275°F (140°C), and line a baking tray with a piece of good-quality greaseproof paper.

Put the egg whites into a clean bowl with the salt and whisk on high speed until they start to become frothy. Then, little by little, tablespoon by tablespoon, add the sugar, whisking all the time. When all the sugar is incorporated, beat in the remaining ingredients and whisk thoroughly together for 2 minutes.

Using 2 tablespoons, put a large blodge of the pavlova mixture in the middle of the lined baking tray. Smooth this down slightly to make the base, then build up a circle around the edges with further tablespoons of mixture. You want to make a big gâteau with sides. The mixture does spread while baking, so make allowances for this!

Bake in the pre-heated oven for 1 hour, then turn off the heat and leave the pavlova to get cold in the oven.

Meanwhile, make the stewed pears for the topping. Peel, core and slice the pears and put in a saucepan with the sugar, butter and sherry. Stew until soft, about 30 minutes. Liquidise, pass through a sieve and leave to cool.

To serve – and do not fill the pavlova base more than 1 hour before serving as it would soften – mound the stewed pears in the middle of the pavlova and top with the cream, whipped until thick. Cut into wedge-shaped portions.

SHOPPING LIST

Fishmonger
1 lb (450 g) smoked haddock fillet
1 lb (450 g) fresh salmon
8 oz (225 g) fillet of sole

Baker
bread for croûtons

Grocer
2 teaspoons white (distilled malt)
  vinegar
14 oz (400 g) butter
1¼ pints (750 ml) milk
1 pint (600 ml) double cream
3–4 medium eggs
4 teaspoons cornflour
1 lb (450 g) caster sugar
8 oz (225 g) frozen spinach
12 oz (350 g) frozen *petits pois*
½ teaspoon vanilla essence

Greengrocer
1 lb (450 g) small potatoes
1¼ lb (550 g) carrots
6 oz (175 g) onions
¼ iceberg lettuce
3 sprigs of parsley
2 tablespoons chives
12 mint leaves, plus 4 sprigs
2 lb (900 g) ripe pears
1 orange

Off-licence
5 fl oz (150 ml) Noilly Prat
5 fl oz (150 ml) white wine
2 tablespoons sweet sherry

Health-food shop (or similar)
1 tablespoon dried elderflowers

Store-cupboard
salt and freshly ground black
  pepper
6 black peppercorns
freshly grated nutmeg

Autumn Menu Three

Salmon Soup with Chopped Red Pepper,
Celery and Dill

•

Baked Fillets of Sole with Mushroom and Apple
accompanied by
White Cabbage with Bacon and Walnut
Dauphinoise Potatoes

•

Blackberry Creams

———————————— • ————————————

*O*nce again, I've chosen a fish soup to be followed by a fish main course, but the combination is a good one, I think.

The soup is cheap to make, although it's rather an unpleasant task taking the meat off the heads. It's also very nourishing, both because of the fish itself and because of the bones which are liquidised and then sieved. Bones are full of calcium which we need for our own bones and our teeth. Of course, sieve the soup very carefully. Garnish as you like, but I'm very much in favour of the texture and colour of the red pepper, celery and dill.

The main course is very tasty, if lacking a little in colour, so you might like to use the peas recipe from p. 141 to brighten it all up a little. I occasionally serve selected fish dishes with a lemon butter twirl, and the rolled sole would benefit from this. Simply mix the juice and finely grated rind of 1 lemon with 6 oz (175 g) soft butter, pipe into six stars (using a star nozzle) on to a tray and chill in the fridge until set. Use as a garnish for the fish at the very last moment. (Other flavourings could be used in the same way – garlic, tomato purée, herbs, etc. – and you could roll the butter into a sausage and chill or freeze, cutting off slices.)

The cabbage dish could be made with green cabbage if you wanted – it's certainly more colourful. I always hope there will be some cabbage left over as it is delicious the next day combined with mashed potatoes, shaped into flat cakes and pan-fried – an up-market bubble and squeak! The potatoes too are wonderful. Before I became slightly diet-conscious, I used to make these using double cream and eggs. Although I did enjoy devouring them, they were sinful for the ever-expanding waistline. I now actually use skimmed milk myself.

The pudding is delicious and deliciously simple. And once again, you should try to pick the blackberries yourself from fields and hedgerows far from main roads. These berries, despite the stained and pricked fingers, always taste so much better than those bought in punnets or those on pick-your-own farms (which are covered in fertilisers and de-bugging sprays).

White cabbage with bacon and walnut

Most folk my age will have horrible memories of overcooked smelly cabbage slopped up (you can't use the word *'served'*) on school dinner plates. It was cooked for an age and a half, having neither life nor colour left in it! This dish is much more delicious, and I personally prefer to use the firm white variety of cabbage.

*4 oz (100 g) smoked bacon,
  finely diced*
2 tablespoons olive oil
*1 lb (450 g) white cabbage, off
  the stalk and finely shredded*

*2 oz (50 g) shelled walnuts,
  chopped*
freshly ground black pepper

Cook the bacon in the oil until nearly crisp, and then add the shredded cabbage. Stir, making sure that everything is coated with the oil and bacon fat, then cook for 10 minutes. Cool, and keep in the fridge until you wish to serve.

Transfer to an ovenproof dish and add the walnuts and black pepper to taste. Heat through in the oven for 20 minutes at the same temperature as the fish – gas mark 4, 350°F (180°C).

Previous page: Baked fillets of sole served with White cabbage with bacon and walnut and Dauphinoise potatoes.

Dauphinoise potatoes

The mistake that most people make when preparing this dish is that they tend to stack rather than spread their potatoes. This means that only the honoured few get the lovely crisp brown top bits. If the dish is done my way, everyone gets a share.

You need a flameproof dish of about 10 in (25 cm) in diameter and 2 in (5 cm) deep.

2 lb (900 g) potatoes
1 garlic clove, peeled and lightly crushed
½ oz (15 g) soft butter
salt and freshly ground black pepper

6 oz (175 g) good strong cheese (I like Gruyère), finely grated
15 fl oz (450 ml) boiling milk (skimmed or otherwise)

Peel the potatoes and slice them carefully and evenly to ⅛ in (3 mm) thickness. Put into cold water; then, when you want to use, drain and pat dry.

Rub the baking dish with the lightly crushed garlic, followed by the butter, covering the base and sides. Spread in half of the dried potatoes, season well and sprinkle with half the cheese. Cover with the remaining potatoes and do likewise with the seasoning and remaining cheese.

Pour on the boiling milk and place your dish on your hot hob. When simmering put into the pre-heated oven – at the same temperature as for the fish and cabbage, gas mark 4, 350°F (180°C) – and bake for 1 hour. Time the potatoes to be ready just 10 minutes before you want to serve them, as they should be put to one side in the warm kitchen to settle, covered loosely with a piece of foil.

Blackberry creams

The blackberry purée can be prepared the day before, but I would make up the cream on the day of the party itself.

8 oz (225 g) blackberries, washed
2 oz (50 g) soft brown sugar
1 tablespoon Crème de Cassis

10 fl oz (300 ml) double cream
2 tablespoons Drambuie
2 free-range egg whites

Place the blackberries, sugar and Cassis in a pan and cook just until the juices start to run. Liquidise, then pass through a coarse sieve into a large clean bowl.

Beat the cream in a separate bowl until it holds soft peaks. Add the Drambuie and then, little by little, beat in the blackberry purée.

In another bowl, beat the egg whites until the same texture as the cream. Fold into the cream mixture. Divide between 6 glass dishes or glasses – saucer champagne glasses are ideal – and chill.

Previous page: Blackberry creams decorated with extra twirls of cream and mint sprigs.

SHOPPING LIST

Fishmonger
2 salmon heads, about 2½ lb
  (1.1 kg)
bones from 12 filleted plaice or sole
6 × 6 oz (175 g) fillets of sole

Butcher
4 oz (100 g) smoked bacon

Grocer
2 tablespoons olive oil
8½ oz (240 g) butter
2 eggs
15 fl oz (450 ml) milk
10 fl oz (300 ml) double cream
6 oz (175 g) strong cheese (such as
  Gruyère)
1 × 8 oz (225 g) can red salmon
2 oz (50 g) shelled walnuts
2 oz (50 g) soft brown sugar

Greengrocer
2 lb (900 g) potatoes
1 lb (450 g) white cabbage
6 oz (175 g) onions
9 oz (250 g) celery
4 oz (100 g) each of carrots and
  fennel
½ red pepper
4 oz (100 g) mushrooms
1 garlic clove
1 leek
fresh dill
6 large sprigs parsley
8 oz (225 g) blackberries
1 apple
1 lemon

Off-licence
10 fl oz (300 ml) dry white wine
1 tablespoon Crème de Cassis
2 tablespoons Drambuie

Store-cupboard
salt and freshly ground black
  pepper

WINTER

$\mathcal{I}$ love the atmosphere of the run-up to Christmas and, when at home, I do my usual MGM number and decorate every single part of the farm with trees, large or small, gilded and silvered branches, and festoons of holly, ivy, baubles, coloured tinsel and artificial robins. I do the same to my seasonal tables, using red and green as my colours. I hope you agree with me that it is one time of year when if you've got it flaunt it!

I also love the food at this time of year. With the long cold nights, I like comforting casseroles, winter vegetables, hot puds and custard . . . and hot toddies. Thus the winter themes are casseroles and sponge puddings, plus puff pastry to be used in starters. Once you have mastered the latter, you have a galaxy of entertaining possibilities, for it can of course make sweet things as well.

WINES FOR WINTER PARTIES

The casseroles are quite bold – one with cider and sage, one with stout, and one with port! Although I am not a lover of Beaujolais Nouveau – it is a real PR hype – it would go happily with such dishes. However, I think an earthy red Loire such as a Chinon would fit the bill or, because I am such a lover of the wines made by the house of Antinori of Florence, one of their true Chiantis.

Most wine experts recommend a dry white wine with a rich pâté and, although I have tried it, it doesn't work for me. To go with all the rich starters, I would opt for an inexpensive Traminer or Gewürztraminer from Alsace. Those from the house of Hugel are always reliable.

·As a welcoming drink, how about your favourite mulled wine with tangerine segments studded with cloves floating therein, and a delicate use of cinnamon sticks as an additional warming feature.

I can't honestly recommend a wine to go with the hot old-fashioned puds, but you could pass around a bottle of KWV brandy – it is very smooth, extremely warming and quite delicious!

Winter Menu One

Marsala Chicken Livers in Puff Pastry
with Greek Yoghurt and Marjoram

•

Pork Chops Braised in Cider with Apples
accompanied by
Spiced Red Cabbage
Grated Courgettes with Walnut and Orange
Danish Glazed Potato Balls

•

Chocolate Marmalade Hazelnut Pudding

---

*T*his is the menu I would choose for a very special winter entertaining occasion. It's memorable, tasty and very easy to do. I would even serve it for Christmas lunch or dinner – you can get a little jaded with the eternal turkey leftovers.

If you've never tried making puff pastry, once you've read the recipe (see p. 245) and watched me demonstrating it in the television series, you will realise that, done *my* way, it's really not so difficult. Once mastered, puff pastry recipes always bring critical acclaim from guests, and it's well worth the time spent and mess created. (Well, *I* make a mess when making it; you may be a much tidier and more meticulous person!) The main things to remember with puff pastry, and I can't emphasise these too often, are that it must be well chilled and it must be brought back to its original, pre-chilling texture before you start rolling it out.

Obviously you can make the starter pastry in the conventional puffed-up way (see p. 188), but you should try these crisp, melt-in-the-mouth 'biscuits'.

Nobody seems to use chicken livers much, but they're inexpensive, very tasty and so easy and quick to cook. I like using the yoghurt with them in the starter recipe as, although the dish is pretty rich, it isn't over the top with calories. But you can use many other fillings instead of the chicken livers – one of the three pâtés on pp. 188, 204 and 209, for instance, or the fillings on pp. 32 and 222.

The pork chop dish has to be one of my great favourites, and it's a boon to a busy host or hostess. I like pork very much, and have fond memories of it when I was a kid, especially at this time of year. Pork was often on the menu during the festive season.

The only thing to watch with the pudding is where you keep it overnight, as in no way do you want the chocolate to start to set. The only alternative would be to prepare and cook it just prior to the party, but that's defeating the object a little. What I would suggest is that you test the pud out a week or so before the party, following the recipe to a T, and see how it turns out. That should help to avoid disaster.

Marsala chicken livers in puff pastry with Greek yoghurt and marjoram

If you liked, you could heat the 'biscuits' of puff pastry through briefly in the oven before filling, but I rather like the contrast of hot filling and cold pastry.

12 Puff pastry 'biscuits' (see opposite)

Chicken liver filling

12 oz (350 g) fresh chicken livers

4 tablespoons olive oil

4 oz (100 g) onions, peeled and finely chopped

salt and freshly ground black pepper (or coriander seeds if you like)

a generous sprinkling of Marsala or sherry

5 fl oz (150 ml) Greek yoghurt mixed with ½ teaspoon cornflour

2 tablespoons chopped fresh marjoram (if available, or parsley, mint or chives)

When you buy your chicken livers, look over them with care and, if there are any signs of yellow, cut out with small scissors. Chop the livers up into smallish cubes, cover with cling film and put in the fridge.

Just prior to sitting down for dinner, heat the olive oil in a pan and cook the onions until golden. Add the chicken livers, salt, pepper and an over-the-top sprinkling of booze of your choice. Stir until the livers look cooked (2–4 minutes), then stir in the yoghurt. (This will not 'split' as it has the cornflour as a stabilising agent.) Leave for up to 10 minutes on a low heat, then stir in the chopped fresh herbs at the last minute.

Arrange 6 of the cooked Puff pastry 'biscuits' on individual serving plates, spoon on the filling and put on the 6 remaining biscuits as 'lids'. Serve at once.

Previous page: A festive table for a seasonal lunch or dinner celebration. The starter is Marsala chicken livers in Puff pastry, garnished with a few salad leaves.

Puff pastry 'biscuits'

1 lb (450 g) Puff pastry
  (see p. 245)
flour for dusting

Roll out the pastry on a well-floured surface to ⅛ in (3 mm) thickness. For this particular dish I use a very large oval cutter (remember that puff pastry always shrinks a little when cooked). Cut out 12 shapes, then transfer to baking trays lined with good-quality greaseproof paper.

Pre-heat the oven to gas mark 8, 450°F (230°C).

Normally one would use one oval for each person because, if it were to be cooked in the conventional way, the puff pastry would puff. However, being slightly perverse, I occasionally like my puff pastry *not* to rise but to bake hard and crisp like a biscuit (but see p. 188 for the puffing variety!). To get this effect, you have to put another sheet of greaseproof paper on your cut-out shapes and then another baking tray on top. Return to the fridge to chill.

When required for cooking, bake in the pre-heated oven, still with the second baking tray on top, for 15 minutes. Remove from the oven and transfer the crisp ovals to cooling trays.

Pork chops braised in cider with apples

This pork chop dish is really delicious although quite cheeky, as it is prepared way ahead of time. I am very lucky with my supplier of pork who has been lauded nationally by foodies – Mr Woodall of Wabberthwaite here in the English Lakes. Having 'developed a relationship with your butcher', look for fresh youngish pork which should be very pale pink in colour with white fat and a smooth thin rind. (The latter is not used in this dish, but can be cut off, cut up and fried to extract the fat.) Off the bone and after skinning, you should aim for an 8 oz (225 g) chop per person.

6 pork chops, about 1 in
  (2.5 cm) thick, weighing about
  8 oz (225 g) each after boning
  and skinning
10 fl oz (300 ml) cider
2 oz (50 g) plain flour
salt and freshly ground black
  pepper

3 tablespoons olive oil
2 oz (50 g) butter
1½ lb (700 g) cooking apples,
  peeled, cored and thinly sliced
12 fresh sage leaves

Remove any fat from the chops, then place in one layer in a suitable dish. Cover with the cider and marinate for 4 days in the fridge. If you feel aghast at the thought of salmonella, or a guest taking ill when eating such 'old' meat, do not worry. When marinating, provided you put the meat and marinade into airtight containers and leave for the full period *in the fridge*, they will come to no harm, but be enhanced as they soak up the cider. I take the container out each day and turn the chops.

Pre-heat the oven to gas mark 4, 350°F (180°C).

Remove the chops from the marinade (which you keep), and pat dry. Season the flour with salt and pepper, and coat the chops with this. Heat

Pork chops braised in cider with apples, accompanied by Spiced red cabbage, Grated courgettes with walnut and orange, and Danish glazed potato balls.

the oil and butter together in the smallest frying-pan you have and, when it is sizzling and singing to you (and not before), fry 2 chops at a time until sealed on both sides and edges. Where people go wrong when they make this type of dish is that they tend to use the largest frying-pan in the house, plonk all 6 chops together into simmering fat and then wonder why the end result is disappointing. The chops will *stew* or *steam* rather than seal.

Butter a suitable roasting dish and line it with the apple slices. Pat the sealed chops dry on kitchen paper and place on top of the apples. Season lightly, pour the marinade over and top each chop with 2 sage leaves.

Cover the dish with a lid or foil and bake in the pre-heated oven for 2 hours. Leave to go cold and then put in the fridge until the next day.

To finish the dish off, put it in the oven pre-heated to gas mark 6, 400°F (200°C), but *uncovered*, and it will take 20–30 minutes to be ready for serving. (Or, put it in at gas mark 4, 350°F/180°C for longer.)

Spiced red cabbage

Any left over from this dish can be fried up the next day using your favourite French dressing instead of butter or oil.

2 oz (50 g) butter
2 tablespoons honey
2 tablespoons olive oil
1 lb (450 g) red cabbage, stalk removed and very finely shredded
6 oz (175 g) onions, peeled and finely chopped

2 garlic cloves, peeled and crushed with 1 teaspoon salt
freshly ground black pepper
¼ teaspoon each of freshly grated nutmeg, ground allspice, cinnamon, dried thyme and caraway seeds
5 fl oz (150 ml) red wine
2 tablespoons wine vinegar

Melt the butter, honey and oil together in a small pan.

Combine all the remaining ingredients, including the cabbage but excluding the wine and vinegar, in a large plastic bowl. Pour the melted honey liquid over the cabbage and mix it all together well. Put into a suitably sized casserole and cover with a lid. This can be done in the morning.

When ready to cook, pre-heat the oven to gas mark 4, 350°F (180°C). Pour the red wine and vinegar into the casserole, mix well and put into the pre-heated oven. It will be ready in an hour. Stir occasionally.

Grated courgettes with walnut and orange

Stir-frying is a quick, easy and delicious way of cooking many veg, particularly courgettes or zucchini. You could also cook them with the finely grated rind and juice of a lime or lemon, but weigh up first whether these sharper citric flavours will go with the main course.

8–12 oz (225–350 g) courgettes, wiped, topped and tailed

finely grated rind and juice of 1 orange
4 tablespoons walnut oil

Coarsely grate the courgettes into a bowl, mix in the rind and juice of the orange and set aside, covered with cling film, in the fridge.

When ready to cook, squeeze the grated courgettes fairly dry. Heat the oil over a low heat, and stir-fry the courgettes for about 4–5 minutes.

Danish glazed potato balls

For this dish to work, you will need a *large*-gauge Parisian scoop, one that is about 1 in (2.5 cm) in diameter. Scoop out balls from the peeled potatoes, about four per person. (The remains of the potatoes can be cooked and mashed for the family next day.)

*6 oz (175 g) dark dessert
chocolate, broken into pieces
4 tablespoons cooking brandy
8 oz (225 g) soft butter
8 oz (225 g) soft brown sugar
3 medium, fresh, free-range
eggs, lightly beaten*

*2 generous tablespoons orange
marmalade
8 oz (225 g) self-raising flour
2 oz (50 g) ground hazelnuts
whipped sweetened double
cream or runny custard
(see p. 108) to serve*

When cooking with chocolate you should *never* melt it simply by putting it into a saucepan over heat (yes, I know you clever folk who sport new-fangled microwaves will be saying it melts in the microwave in a minute – but who wants to spend all that money purely to melt chocolate?). It has to be placed in a bowl with some liquid – in this case the cooking brandy. (If you haven't any cooking brandy, make sure next time you go away on holiday that you snap up some of those miniature orange-flavoured liqueurs often handed out on the plane with coffee!) Then the bowl should be set over a saucepan of simmering, *not* boiling, water and the chocolate allowed to melt gently. Remove from the heat and leave to cool.

Cream together the soft butter and sugar – I find that the warmth of my hand helps to get this off to a good start – and then, little by little, add the lightly beaten eggs. Do take time and trouble with this, otherwise your mixture could split. It should be light and fluffy. Fold in the marmalade and cooled melted chocolate, then cover with cling film and leave some-where warm until you wish to bake it.

When you want to cook, pre-heat the oven to gas mark 4, 350°F (180°C).

Simply fold the self-raising flour and ground hazelnuts into the choco-late mixture, then pour into a greased dish measuring 10 × 8 in (25 × 20 cm) and spread out evenly. Bake in the pre-heated oven for 1 hour. Serve hot with cream or custard.

SHOPPING LIST

Butcher

12 oz (350 g) fresh chicken livers

6 pork chops, about 8 oz (225 g) each after boning and skinning

Grocer

about 6 fl oz (175 ml) olive oil

4 tablespoons walnut oil

2 tablespoons wine vinegar

12 oz (350 g) butter

8 oz (225 g) margarine

8 oz (225 g) shortening or white lard

10 fl oz (300 ml) double cream (or custard ingredients, see p. 108)

3 medium eggs

5 fl oz (150 ml) Greek yoghurt

1 lb (450 g) strong plain flour

8 oz (225 g) self-raising flour

2 oz (50 g) plain flour

½ teaspoon cornflour

2 oz (50 g) ground hazelnuts

6 oz (175 g) dark dessert chocolate

9 oz (250 g) soft brown sugar

2 tablespoons orange marmalade

2 tablespoons honey

Greengrocer

1¾ lb (800 g) old potatoes

1 lb (450 g) red cabbage

8–12 oz (225–350 g) courgettes

10 oz (275 g) onions

2 garlic cloves

2 tablespoons fresh marjoram (or parsley, mint or chives)

12 fresh sage leaves

1½ lb (700 g) cooking apples

1 orange

1 lemon

Off-licence

Marsala or sherry

10 fl oz (300 ml) cider

5 fl oz (150 ml) red wine

4 tablespoons cooking brandy

Store-cupboard

salt and freshly ground black pepper

freshly grated nutmeg

ground allspice, cinnamon, dried thyme, caraway seeds

Puff pastry vol-au-vents

—————•—————

1 lb (450 g) Puff pastry
  (see p. 245)
flour for dusting

1 free-range egg, beaten with
  1 teaspoon water, to glaze

Roll out the pastry (once it has reached the correct temperature) on a floured surface to ¼ in (5 mm) thickness. Cut into 6 of the shapes you prefer – medium rounds, ovals or diamonds – then, using a very sharp knife, trace a line about ½ in (1 cm) from the edge of the shape, without cutting all the way through the pastry. Place on a slightly dampened baking tray. Put back into the fridge to chill for about 30 minutes.

Meanwhile pre-heat the oven to gas mark 8, 450°F (230°C).

Very lightly brush the tops of the pastry shapes with the egg wash, avoiding the cut edges as the wash would prevent them from rising.

Bake the shapes in the pre-heated oven for 30 minutes. Remove from the oven and use a knife to remove the incised smaller shapes on the top. Scoop out any damp or greasy pastry. Put the pastry shapes back in the oven for a few minutes to get them really crisp, then leave to cool in the switched-off oven. *But* constantly check to avoid burning. When cool, fill with the filling of your choice, and top with the 'hats' if you like.

You can bake the shapes as they are, then cut in half horizontally before crisping in the oven. Put the filling in between the two layers.

Rich pâté

—————•—————

I always have a pot of pâté in the fridge for that odd snack lunch, or to use if somebody calls in unexpectedly. It can swiftly be piped on to

Previous page: A cosy formal dinner for winter in front of a blazing fire. The starter is Puff pastry vol-au-vents filled with Rich pâté and served with Madeira sauce.

small savoury biscuits or mini round croûtons (see p. 248). It is excellent piped into walnut-sized twirls and served with grilled steak, and another unusual way of using it is in small round éclairs with a touch of Bovril on the top (see p. 68 for a choux pastry éclair recipe).

12 oz (350 g) chicken livers, cleaned and roughly chopped	2 oz (50 g) smoked bacon, rinded and finely diced
4 tablespoons sherry, brandy or Marsala	2 oz (50 g) onions, peeled and finely chopped
1 oz (25 g) duck fat or butter	chopped fresh marjoram to taste
	4 tablespoons double cream

Marinate the cleaned, prepared chicken livers in the booze of your choice for at least 24 hours, turning them over once or twice.

Melt the duck fat or butter in a saucepan and cook off the bacon until well done. Add the onions and cook until nice and golden. Add the chicken livers and booze along with the marjoram and cook for 15 minutes.

Cool, then liquidise with the double cream. Either pot in ramekins or leave in a covered dish so that you can pipe it into the cold Puff pastry vol-au-vents (see preceding recipe). Pipe cold into the hollow vol-au-vents, or on to the bottoms of the pastry shapes and top with the tops. Serve with hot Madeira sauce.

Madeira sauce

This is easy. Simply boil 5 fl oz (150 ml) Madeira to reduce down to a couple of tablespoons, then stir into 10 fl oz (300 ml) Gravy (see p. 249). Serve hot with the filled Puff pastry vol-au-vents.

Beef casserole with stout

Casseroles are comforting cuisine, but are sometimes maligned by the so-called foodies. Many consider them 'cheap', as tougher cuts of meat are often used; some say they would never serve them at a dinner party. Sad, I say, because they are marvellous for relaxed entertaining.

6 good sirloin steaks, weighing about 6 oz (175 g) each
freshly ground black pepper
1 heaped tablespoon wholemeal flour
2 oz (50 g) soft butter
2 tablespoons olive oil or Garlic oil (see p. 250)

6 oz (175 g) each of onions, carrots, celery and turnips, peeled and finely diced
juice and grated rind of 2 oranges
10 fl oz (300 ml) bottled stout
5 fl oz (150 ml) red wine
1 heaped tablespoon demerara sugar
fresh parsley

Pre-heat the oven to gas mark 3, 325°F (160°C).

Dry the steaks well and season generously with freshly ground pepper. Lightly coat with the flour.

Combine the butter and oil in a frying-pan and heat until sizzling. *One by one* seal the steaks on both sides in the fat, then remove from the pan and put to one side. Cook the diced vegetables in the fat remaining in the pan, adding some of the orange juice if necessary.

Lay the steaks flat in one layer in a casserole and cover with the vegetables, remaining orange juice and grated rind, stout and red wine. Sprinkle on the demerara sugar.

Cover, place in the pre-heated oven and cook for 1½ hours. Or, if you want to prepare in advance, cook for 1¼ hours only, then re-heat, at the same temperature, for 30 minutes. Garnish with parsley.

Previous page: Beef casserole with stout, accompanied by Mashed pumpkin with sweet potato and a Winter salad.

Mashed pumpkin with sweet potato

The combination of these two vegetables makes a happy marriage which can be enhanced with a touch of powdered ginger as well if you like. Cooked in the morning, they can easily be re-heated in a bowl over a saucepan of simmering water for 20 minutes.

1 lb (450 g) pumpkin, peeled, seeded and coarsely but evenly chopped

8 oz (225 g) sweet potato, peeled and likewise chopped
salt and freshly ground black pepper
2 oz (50 g) soft butter

Place both vegetables in a large saucepan, cover with approximately 3 pints (1.8 litres) cold water and add a little runny salt. Bring to the boil and then cook until quite soft (about 20 minutes). Strain and return to the stove.

Add the butter to the pan and heat until it melts. Remove from the heat and, using a masher, pound until coarsely bound together. Season with freshly ground black pepper and a little more salt. Cool, and then cover with cling film until you need to re-heat (see above).

Winter salad

Don't add the walnuts to the salad until the last minute, as otherwise they tend to become grey-looking. If preparing the major proportion of the salad a little in advance, you will need to put lemon juice on the apple pieces to prevent them going brown. Try to get apples with an orange or red tinge to the skin as this adds colour to the salad. Coarsely grated carrots, courgettes or turnips could also be used in a winter salad.

8 oz (225 g) young Brussels
  sprouts (prepared weight)
8 oz (225 g) white of leek
  (prepared weight)
4 oz (100 g) dried apricots
2 unpeeled Cox's apples,
  quartered and cored
juice of ½ lemon (if necessary)

2 tablespoons chopped parsley
sea salt to taste
3 oz (75 g) shelled walnuts,
  chopped
about 3 fl oz (85 ml) French
  dressing (see p. 240)

Shred the sprouts finely and place in a large salad bowl. Slice the leeks finely, separate them into rings and place in the bowl. Chop the apricots and apples into small pieces and add to the bowl as well (leave the skin on the apples and coat with lemon juice if necessary).

Add the parsley, salt and chopped walnuts just before tossing with the dressing. Serve immediately.

A nice flavour could be given to the dressing for this salad by adding the finely grated rind and juice of a lemon.

Citrus syrup hazelnut sponge pud

•

When I was a child, my Nan used to multiply this recipe by four or more and cook an enormous pudding in those lovely old-fashioned cream (outside) and white (inside) mixing bowls in the boiler in the wash-house. It was eagerly devoured by the family with lashings of home-made custard. The next day, cold slices were thickly buttered and put in our lunch boxes, or were fried for high tea in butter until slightly brown, then had more golden syrup poured over.

Nowadays I just make this 2-pint (1.1-litre) version, which is always appreciated by my guests, and I serve it with a rich home-made Orange custard to which I have indulgently added a couple of tablespoons of

A wedge of Citrus syrup hazelnut sponge pud, served with Orange custard.

cooking brandy (see p. 108) and, yes, with a dish of whipped, lightly sugared double cream as well! My guests leave the house with a lovely warm, glowing feeling to counteract the misty, murky, night air!

just over 4 oz (100 g) butter
3 tablespoons golden syrup
2 tablespoons ground hazelnuts
finely grated rind of 1 orange
4 oz (100 g) caster sugar

2 medium free-range eggs,
* lightly beaten*
4 oz (100 g) self-raising flour
juice and finely grated rind of
* 1 lemon*
Orange custard (see p. 108) to
* serve*

Very lightly grease your 2-pint (1.1-litre) pudding basin with a tiny knob of the butter. Spoon in the syrup, then mix in the ground hazelnuts and orange rind.

In a separate mixing bowl, beat the remaining butter and the sugar until light and fluffy in consistency and white in colour. Little by little, beat in the eggs – do please remember to take care and time with this, otherwise your mixture could split or curdle. Lightly fold in the self-raising flour and lemon juice and rind. Top the syrup mix in the basin with this sponge, level the surface, then cover with a double thickness of foil or greaseproof paper. Secure well with string.

Have to hand a saucepan which will hold the pudding basin comfortably, and in it bring to the boil enough water to come about half-way up the sides of the basin. Put the pudding basin in the pan, cover the pan and cook for 2 hours. Do check from time to time to see that your base pan still has water in it!

Remove the basin from the pan, take off the foil or paper and test with a knife point that the pud is cooked (the point should come out dry). Then leave, covered with the foil again, for 10 minutes to rest. Turn out on to a large serving dish, and slice into 6 devilish portions. I have no idea of the calorie count!

Hand the custard (and/or cream if you wish) separately.

SHOPPING LIST

Butcher
12 oz (350 g) chicken livers
6 good sirloin steaks, about 6 oz
  (175 g) each
2 oz (50 g) smoked bacon

Grocer
about 12 fl oz (350 ml) olive oil
about 8 oz (225 g) butter
1 oz (25 g) duck fat (or butter)
8 oz (225 g) margarine
8 oz (225 g) shortening or white
  lard
9 eggs
12 fl oz (350 ml) double cream,
  plus an extra 10 fl oz (300 ml) to
  serve with the pud if liked
10 fl oz (300 ml) single cream
1–2 tablespoons wine vinegar
1 lb (450 g) strong plain flour
1 tablespoon wholemeal flour
4 oz (100 g) self-raising flour
2 teaspoons cornflour
5 oz (150 g) caster sugar
1 tablespoon demerara sugar
3 tablespoons golden syrup
2 tablespoons ground hazelnuts
4 oz (100 g) dried apricots
3 oz (75 g) shelled walnuts

Greengrocer
1 lb (450 g) pumpkin
8 oz (225 g) sweet potato
12 oz (350 g) young Brussels
  sprouts
8 oz (225 g) white of leek
8 oz (225 g) onions
6 oz (175 g) each of carrots, celery
  and turnips
12–15 garlic cloves
fresh marjoram
2 tablespoons parsley
6 oranges
2–3 lemons
2 Cox's apples

Off-licence
4 tablespoons sherry, brandy or
  Marsala
5 fl oz (150 ml) Madeira
10 fl oz (300 ml) bottled stout
5 fl oz (150 ml) red wine
2 tablespoons cooking brandy

Store-cupboard
10 fl oz (300 ml) Gravy (see p. 249)
sea salt and freshly ground black
  pepper
½ teaspoon dry English mustard
  powder

tray and lay the gammon steaks flat down on it. Bake for 20 minutes.

Cut the hole in the pineapple rings a little larger than normal and place a ring on top of each steak. Pop back in the oven for 5 minutes.

Break an egg into each pineapple ring and return to the oven for a further 10 minutes. You'll lose some white, inevitably, but on the whole it looks good and tastes divine!

Potato, cheese, sultana and walnut bread

Few people in their right mind would even contemplate getting up on a morning when they are having a brunch party and baking bread! (Especially if, as in my case, the night before has been fun but far too much juice from the grape has been consumed!) I do hope I can persuade you, however, that this bread takes very little effort and hardly any time and, when accompanied by some of your locally made cheese, brings the meal to a splendid ending.

Start off about 1¼ hours before you plan to sit down to your first brunch course.

4 oz (100 g) Cheddar cheese
2 garlic cloves, peeled and
 crushed with 2 teaspoons salt
12 oz (350 g) self-raising flour
12 oz (350 g) potatoes, peeled
2 oz (50 g) sultanas

2 oz (50 g) shelled walnuts,
 chopped
2 free-range eggs, lightly beaten
5 oz (150 g) natural or Greek
 yoghurt

Pre-heat the oven to gas mark 5, 375°F (190°C).

Coarsely grate the cheese into a large mixing bowl and add the garlic and flour. Grate the potatoes coarsely into the bowl too, and add the sultanas and nuts. Get your hands in and make sure all the ingredients are evenly distributed, then add the eggs and yoghurt. Mix slowly to a dough – a relatively simple but ever so 'clarty' task.

Turn out on to a generously floured baking tray, shape into a circle and lightly flatten down. Make wedge indentations with a palette knife where you plan to slice. Bake in the pre-heated oven for 1 hour. Test for 'doneness' by inserting a metal skewer; it will come out quite clean and dry if the bread is ready. (If it's still a bit damp, cook for a little longer.)

Remove from the oven and put on a serving dish lightly covered with foil. Needless to say, your local cheeses should be out and airing at this stage . . . as well as lashings of soft, preferably unsalted, butter.

Drinks for a brunch party

Without any doubt, a brunch has to start off with a Buck's Fizz; it must be made with beautiful fresh orange juice, but you can economise on the type of sparkling wine you then add (see p. 113). Keep the oranges in the warm kitchen overnight then, before squeezing, roll them on the work surface; this makes them more juicy. There are occasions when I really do enjoy a glass of peach champagne, a drink much derided by the so-called intelligent wine critics. (I just say a little of what you fancy is better than something you don't care for that they recommend!) Try it once and I am sure you will like it.

To be on the safe side, and to go with all the courses, I would settle for a decent *rosé*. The ever-popular Anjou *rosé* from the Loire is a pleasant little wine, and so are many of the New World Blanc de Noir varieties.

For those who don't want alcohol, or who want *both*, make some proper coffee. It's very important that you find yourself a good supplier, one who stocks breakfast coffees, after-dinner coffees, different beans and different roasts, etc. There are many ways of making coffee and everyone claims theirs is the best. What I do is put 4 oz (100 g) ground coffee from sealed packets into a jug and pour on up to 3 pints (1.8 litres) water off the boil. Stir with a wooden spoon and leave for 5 minutes. Pour into cups through a fine sieve.

If you are having your brunch in the summer, and it is a lovely hot day, end the meal with *iced* coffee to which you have added a little Frangelico!

VEGETARIAN BUFFET

Mini Red Pepper and Onion Wholemeal Quiches
Courgette and Mint Roll with Savoury Cheese Stuffing
Baked Red Peppers with Tomato Provençale
Pea and Peanut Salad with Roquefort Cheese
and Chive Balls
Baby Sweetcorn in Mustard and Honey Dressing
Layered Peach, Cucumber, Pepper and Sunflower
Seed Salad with Hot Walnut Honey Dressing
French Bean and Orange Salad

When the producer of the television series first suggested that I do one programme for vegetarians, I put the idea way at the back of my mind, and at subsequent meetings brushed over the subject. When it came to the crunch, though, I had to give in – life, after all, is a series of compromises. I accepted the challenge and actually enjoyed creating the ideas for the recipes and making the programme itself.

I've always cooked with lots of vegetables. A quick look at the shopping lists throughout the book will show how much my style of cooking relies on a good greengrocer. Creating the recipes for this buffet wasn't difficult, nor is the preparation. Everything can be done in advance, and even the salads can be prepared about 2 hours beforehand. You just don't *dress* them until the very last minute.

I love buffet parties – they generate such excitement and spontaneity – and I normally give two a year at the farm. As I love meat, huge sirloins of beef are roasted and served. However, this year I'm planning to shock my bi-annual visitors and give them this purely vegetarian knees-up! Most of the following recipes are for twelve people unless otherwise stated. You could also serve a pud if your guests have a sweet tooth.

The table requires particular attention. I don't like a flat table with flat plates of portioned food. I scatter over the main buffet table an odd selection of boxes and containers and then float over them a cloth (end rolls of cotton, etc., bought from the market in Rawtenstall). Using safety pins, pins, staples, etc., we drape, pin and tuck, to get an overall stunning effect. The dishes are laid out at these different heights, which I think looks *much* more interesting. It's a lot of work (and needs two to do it), but it's still all part of the JT masterplan; I do it the day before the party. However, if you do decide to try this, it is essential that everything is firm and secure. You don't want some idiot heavily helping himself to an item of food and collapsing the whole dish!

Mini red pepper
and onion wholemeal quiches

———————————•———————————

These are obviously a little bit more fiddly to make, but are much more satisfying for a buffet party, and much easier for people to eat than slices from a large quiche. You could use any of your own favourite fillings.

Makes 12

⅔ quantity Wholemeal quiche
  pastry (see p. 247)
flour for dusting

Filling

1 tablespoon vegetable oil
8 oz (225 g) onions, peeled and
  finely chopped

12 oz (350 g) red peppers,
  seeded and diced
12 teaspoons grated Parmesan
  cheese
10 fl oz (300 ml) double cream
2 free-range eggs and 1 egg
  yolk, lightly beaten
1 teaspoon powdered cumin

After the pastry has come back to its soft texture, roll it out on a floured surface to form a large circle. Cut out individual small circles using a fluted cutter. Tins measuring 3 in (7.5 cm) across and 1 in (2.5 cm) deep, will need a cutter of 4 in (10 cm) in diameter, to allow for the sides.

Place these little pastry circles in the tins and drop in individual paper sponge cake liners. Fill these with ceramic beans and leave in the fridge again overnight to settle and chill.

Pre-heat the oven to gas mark 3, 325°F (160°C), and bake the mini quiches blind for at least 20 minutes. Remove from the oven, take out the paper cases and beans, and if you think the pastry could be even drier, put it back in the oven for a few more minutes. Then leave to cool. Turn the oven up to gas mark 5, 375°F (190°C).

Previous page: A sunny buffet spread for vegetarians: Mini red pepper and onion wholemeal quiches, Baked red peppers with Tomato Provençale, Courgette and mint roll, French bean and orange salad, a simple salad of watercress and orange segments, Baby sweetcorn in mustard and honey dressing, Layered peach, cucumber, pepper and sunflower seed salad, Pea and peanut salad with Roquefort cheese and chive balls, and a wonderful punch.

For the filling, heat the oil in a pan and cook the onions and red peppers until soft but not coloured. Spoon these into the mini quiche cases. Mix the remaining ingredients together and pour into the cases, filling them only two-thirds full. Put in the pre-heated oven for about 6–10 minutes, then pull the shelf out and fill the cases with the remainder of the custard – this avoids the custard spilling out and down the sides of the pastry. Bake for another 20–24 minutes – 30 minutes altogether – then remove from the oven if set. Leave to cool.

Courgette and mint roll with savoury cheese stuffing

The first task is to prepare your baking tin which should measure approximately 12 × 9 × 1 in (30 × 23 × 2.5 cm) – a Swiss-roll tin. Get good-quality greaseproof paper and turn the tin *over* so that you can actually see the size of the base. Fold the paper over it so that you get the imprint of the base. Fold in these imprints to get a tin-shaped piece of paper and hold the corners together with staples or paper clips. Turn the tray the right way up and the rectangle of paper will drop in. Grease the paper well with either oil or extra melted butter.

1½ lb (700 g) courgettes
finely grated rind of 2 lemons
4 oz (100 g) butter
at least 40 fresh mint leaves,
 finely chopped
4 medium free-range eggs,
 separated
salt and freshly ground black
 pepper

3 tablespoons freshly grated
 Parmesan cheese
Stuffing
1 lb (450 g) good cream cheese
8 oz (225 g) carrots, peeled and
 finely grated
4 kernels preserved ginger,
 chopped
2 heaped tablespoons finely
 chopped fresh herbs

a lot of oil, but after the peppers have cooked, the oil is drained off and used for French dressings (it will have captured some of the delicious red pepper flavour).

Pre-heat the oven to gas mark 6, 400°F (200°C), and bake the peppers for 1¼ hours. I like them to look slightly black around the edges. Leave to cool and then drain off the oil.

Divide the Tomato provençale between the pepper halves.

Bring the savoury crumb topping ingredients together in the food processor. Divide between the pepper halves. Grill to brown, or heat through in the oven for about 10 minutes. Serve warm, or leave to cool.

Pea and peanut salad with Roquefort cheese and chive balls

My new next-door neighbour at Bowness owns a nut factory. When he offered a few samples, although I hate mixing business with pleasure, I reluctantly agreed. An enormous box duly arrived at the hotel and was plonked into the dry store where it stayed for more weeks than I really care to remember. (Never once did my neighbour ask for my opinion of them!)

One day I went into the dry store and found it not as tidy as it should be, so read the riot act; I stayed there whilst we got all the shelves ship-shape like a well-stocked supermarket and, lo and behold, the peanut box emerged! We opened it and for the next few days had nut-sampling sessions. We were in awe, particularly when we ate his new line of salted honey peanuts. They are the ultimate in nuts and are now used extensively both at the hotel and at home on the farm. They are available in many supermarkets (I'm not allowed to tell you where as the BBC don't let writers share such secrets) and in several health-food stores. Seek them out, do. Buy more than you need for this recipe because they are habit-forming.

8 oz (225 g) frozen petits
  pois, defrosted
salt
12 oz (350 g) salted honey
  peanuts
3 celery stalks, finely chopped
2 red peppers, seeded and finely
  chopped
3 oz (75 g) tiny croûtons (see
  p. 248)

½ iceberg lettuce, finely
  shredded
2 bunches of watercress
**Roquefort cheese and chive
  balls**
6 oz (175 g) Roquefort cheese
6 oz (175 g) good cream cheese
4 tablespoons finely chopped
  fresh chives

Cook the *petits pois* in salted water according to the instructions on the packet, then refresh in cold water, drain and cool.

Make the cheese and chive balls by beating the cheeses together, then forming into balls the size of walnuts. Coat liberally with chives.

Combine all the salad ingredients together on a flat platter and arrange the cheese and chive balls around the edge. The salad needs no dressing and is really delicious.

Baby sweetcorn
in mustard and honey dressing

Small individual packets of baby sweetcorn vary in size, but you should have four tiny corn cobs per person.

48 baby sweetcorn cobs
salt
5 tablespoons runny honey

1 tablespoon dry English
  mustard powder

I usually cut off the ends of the baby corn and then lightly wash in cold water. Cook them in salted water until just becoming tender (about 5

French dressing

There are lots of dressings attached to individual recipes throughout the book, but here I give you the absolute basics. I make my dressings in the blender – by far the easiest way – but of course you can blend a dressing by shaking all the ingredients together in a screw-top jar.

10 fl oz (300 ml) olive oil
½ teaspoon salt

½ teaspoon dry English
  mustard powder
1 tablespoon wine vinegar
½ teaspoon fresh lemon juice

Whizz these together in the blender, and then use that arbiter of kitchen taste – your finger. Dip it in and see what else the basic dressing needs. It could do with some freshly ground black pepper, it could require sweetening with sugar or flavouring with some crushed garlic. I have a sweet tooth, so occasionally I add a little bit of honey. I like to use walnut oil, so often I replace 2 tablespoons of the olive oil with this. (Hazelnut, sesame, etc. – the highly flavoured oils – could be added in the same way.)

The basic oil itself can be varied, according to your palate and pocket. There are fruity extra-virgin olive oils available now, as well as light ones; the unflavoured oils such as grapeseed, corn, safflower, etc., could be appropriate for some uses. The oil left over from cooking the peppers on p. 235 is superb in some dressings; then, so is bacon fat, or the juices left over from cooking a chicken (see p. 70).

The vinegars can be varied as well, but never use malt. There are red and white wine, cider and sherry (even champagne!) vinegars, and a wonderfully fragrant and dark aged vinegar from Italy, balsamic. The tiniest taste – just ½ teaspoon – of a raspberry vinegar can transform a dressing.

Experiment!

Drinks for buffet parties

If your guests don't drink, then home-made lemonade is easy to make and serve. On a cold day, stock made from vegetables is quite nice if spiced up with a generous dash of Worcestershire sauce. If they take a *little* alcohol, then Guinness or a really good strong cider could be appropriate.

However, I think the easiest drink at a buffet is a punch. This is much simpler than offering a variety of drinks. I make mine up in a wonderful silver-plated punch bowl I bought for peanuts (well, £80 or so) in a local flea market. Place in your bowl 8 oz (225 g) raspberries that you have puréed and passed through a sieve, along with the juice and finely grated rind of 2 oranges and 4 large sprigs of rosemary. Pour in 2 whole bottles of sparkling white wine and 1 bottle of Sauvignon Blanc from the New World. Add masses of fresh mint and ice cubes. A tip about opening champagne or sparkling wine bottles is to hold the cork in a cloth and *turn the bottle*; this stops the wine from exploding out (or usually does – it didn't quite work on the programme!)

TOVEY'S TIPS

The following recipes are, for me, foundations for good, sound, sensible home entertaining and will, I feel sure, help you all! If you have any queries please drop me a line at Miller Howe, Windermere, English Lakes LA23 1EY.

FARMHOUSE PASTRY

I make no excuses whatsoever for bringing out yet another variation of my grandmother's pastry. Although it is rich and decadent, it always, but always, brings forth groans of appreciation, and requests for the recipe. And forget all those old wives' tales of cold hearts, cold hands and cold slabs – it's the handling of the pastry that counts, and to do it well you've got to be light-hearted and in the right mood. It's a heavy heart, not a cold one, that makes heavy pastry.

Makes about 2 lb (900 g)
12 oz (350 g) self-raising flour
4 oz (100 g) cornflour
12 oz (350 g) soft unsalted butter

4 oz (100 g) soft brown sugar
finely grated rind of 2 oranges
2 medium free-range egg yolks,
*   lightly beaten*

Into a large round-bottomed bowl sift the self-raising flour and the cornflour. On to this break, in walnut-sized bits, the lovely soft butter. If you forget to take the butter out of the fridge in time for it to get soft, *tough* (and your pastry will be likewise). By using *soft* butter you simply spread it smoothly, allowing it to take up the flour in a gentle fashion.

To start with, hold your hands wide open in front of you, put them in the bowl and lightly coat the butter with the flour mix. Then, taking up a handful as high as possible, rub your thumbs over the mix (never allowing it to touch your fingers), and let it all fall back into the bowl. I always demonstrate this with my back to my audience, and they think I am starting to perform the Dance of the Dying Swan! The pastry will begin to feel rather dampish and, as they say in Lancashire, 'clarty'. *Don't overwork it.*

Add the soft brown sugar and grated orange rind and bring together lightly. Then zig-zag the beaten egg yolks over the mix. Hold the bowl up in the air away from you and gently rotate it in circles and shake it up and down – rather as if you were panning for gold! The egg yolk will quickly start to attract small and then bigger lumps of pastry, and quite quickly it will come together.

To make it into 2 balls (1 for the base and 1 for the lid), don't squeeze them like mad to form perfect shapes (you've just spent all that time to get the pastry *light*). Just keep your working hands spread open, and gently coax the dough together. As you do this, memorise what each ball of pastry feels like at this stage. This is what it must feel like the next day when you want to roll and bake it (it'll need about an hour at room temperature). Wrap each ball of pastry in foil and rest overnight in the fridge.

PUFF PASTRY

When the delightful class of seven amateurs was told I was going to show them how to make puff pastry, I could immediately detect their hopes rise, but spirits fall as, time and time again, people say they feel they can't make pastry. I must admit that I find the classic method for this pastry frightfully difficult – so much so that the following is the version we use all the time at Miller Howe. I was determined to have them succeed, and if you watched the television programme you will have been aware of their varying degrees of success. They have, however, all written to me saying that the pastry they took home was delicious!

While we were making the pastry during the shoot, I decided, on the spur of the moment, to have lots of laughs, and the actual rolling-out procedure rather resembled the John Tovey Chorus with me singing (if you can admit that my vocal chords produce such a sound): 'Away – up – back, away – up – back.' At the end of that particular shoot the producer came down on to the floor from the upstairs gallery and said it would have been better suited to an aerobics class.

Normally the making of puff pastry takes hours and hours, for you are forever giving it a roll and a turn and putting it back in the fridge for 30 minutes, repeating this process at least four times, often forgetting just how many turns the ruddy thing has had. This pastry can be done and dusted in only 15 minutes, *but* it is best to prepare two lots of the following recipe as the short spell between rolls does make for a better end texture. In any case, if you are going to make a right mess of the kitchen with one lot, you might as well make double and freeze half!

Once again, it is imperative that you seek out the *strong plain* flour from your grocer as without this the pastry will not be good. Strong flour has a higher gluten content than plain flour, and this enables a flour mixture to rise well.

middle base will come up to the top. Carry on chopping until it is visibly clear that you have got all the ingredients smoothly bound together, and no sign of pockets of flour.

Divide the dough into 3 and carefully and *very gently* form into loose balls. As with all the other pastries, it is imperative that you memorise exactly what the balls feel like at this stage. When you come to roll the pastry out, it must, absolutely must, be the same texture. Place in a plastic bag, tie up, and put in the fridge overnight (or in the freezer).

The next day remove the pastry from the fridge, leave at room temperature for it to come back to that self-same texture, then roll out. To use the pastry for quiches, employ the same techniques as required for lining the base of the Farmhouse pie on p. 22. For individual quiches, see p. 232.

LARGE-BASE CROÛTONS

These can be useful in a great many ways, particularly as the basis of a delicious and simple starter.

Makes 6 croûtons
6 thin slices of bread
3 oz (75 g) butter, melted

Cut as large circles as possible from your slices of bread (leave what is left over in the fridge to make savoury or plain breadcrumbs in the next day or so). Cook them in the melted butter until nice and golden – in a frying-pan if you like, but I think they are much better baked. Simply dunk them into the melted butter, place on a baking tray and bake in an oven pre-heated to gas mark 4, 350°F (180°C), for 30–40 minutes.

Drain on kitchen paper and, when cold, wrap in foil and leave in a cool place. They can be prepared and cooked a day or so in advance.

SMALL CROÛTONS

These can be made the day before your party, or on the morning of the do.

Makes 36 croûtons
3 medium-thick slices of bread

2 tablespoons olive oil
2 oz (50 g) butter

Remove the crusts from the bread and cut the slices into 36 cubes. Heat the olive oil in a frying-pan and add and melt the butter. When sizzling, put in the bread cubes and fry, turning, until brown. You may need to add more oil and butter. Drain on kitchen paper and keep in an airtight jar until needed. Heat the croûtons through slightly in the pre-heating oven before serving.

HOME-MADE STOCK

Stock is a relatively simple item to make and does not necessarily need a meat carcass (although a chicken carcass can be used, making a more richly flavoured stock). An accumulation of clean vegetable peelings (except those from potatoes), outer leaves of lettuce and cauliflower, stalks and leaves from celery, skins from onions (these add colour and flavour), tomatoes and garlic can all be stored in the salad drawer of your fridge. When you have enough, put them in a pan and cover them with cold water. An onion, a couple of bay leaves, a whole carrot or other vegetable you happen to have around, plus some black peppercorns, could be added for extra flavour. Bring to the boil, cover, then *simmer* (never boil) for at least a couple of hours. Strain, cool and keep in the fridge.

GRAVY

The old-fashioned way of making gravy, while excellent, is not for me when I am entertaining, as it infringes on my pleasure! I always make mine the day before by the following method.

Makes about 1½ pints (900 ml)

4 oz (100 g) butter
1 lb (450 g) clean vegetable peelings and chopped root vegetables
4 oz (100 g) plain flour
2 pints (1.2 litres) Home-made stock (see above), preferably made with meat bones of the same type as the meat you are serving
flavouring of your choice (see below)

In a large saucepan melt the butter, add the prepared peelings and chopped vegetables, and cook over a medium to high heat until they are nice and brown. This takes about 20–30 minutes, and you must stir quite roughly from time to time. Turn up the heat as high as possible and add the flour. Cook this, stirring often, for another 10–15 minutes. Add the stock (it will sizzle and bubble like a witch's cauldron), and let the gravy simmer for a further 40 minutes.

Pass through a sieve into a clean container, pushing with a soup ladle, and then the fun starts. The most important thing you need at this stage is your *tasting finger*. By adding tomato purée, mint or redcurrant jelly, mustard, horseradish, Bovril, wine vinegar or honey – or anything you fancy would contribute, even a small square of dark chocolate for colour – you will create a taste that you really enjoy. When you get there, and after the gravy is cold, simply cover it and put in the fridge. It takes hardly any time at all to re-heat in a bowl over simmering water to serve with a roast.

Warm the oil in a large saucepan, add the onions and peppers and cook, stirring all the time, until they absorb the oil. Add the sugar, mix in well and leave to simmer for 1½ hours. Stir every now and again with a wooden spoon to make sure nothing is sticking on the bottom of the pan.

Add the vinegar, a tablespoon or so at a time, stirring vigorously so that it is evenly distributed through the reduced, thick vegetable mixture. Cook for a further 30–45 minutes. Cool, then pot in the usual way.

CURRY ESSENCE

Curry essence is a useful stand-by which can be the flavouring medium of your actual home-made curries, or can be used (in smaller quantities, of course) to spice up cream sauces, hollandaise and mayonnaise.

Makes about 7 fl oz (200 ml)

2 tablespoons olive oil
2 oz (50 g) unsalted butter
4 oz (100 g) onions, peeled and finely chopped
¼ teaspoon ground allspice
2 bay leaves
the seeds from 3 cardamom pods
2 × 1-in (2.5-cm) cinnamon sticks
4 cloves

1 tablespoon coriander seeds
1 teaspoon chilli powder
2 garlic cloves, crushed with ½ teaspoon salt
1 teaspoon mustard seeds
6 black peppercorns
1 teaspoon ground turmeric
5 fl oz (150 ml) red wine
2 tablespoons apricot jam

Heat the oil and butter in a pan and fry the onions until golden. Add all the spices and cook over a high heat for several minutes. Stir well, then add the wine and jam, and simmer for 5 minutes. Liquidise, pass through a coarse sieve and store in a screw-top jar in the fridge.

INDEX

Pages with illustrations are shown in **bold** type.